New Directions in
Labor Economics and
Industrial Relations

New Directions in Labor Economics and Industrial Relations

EDITED BY
Michael J. Carter and
William H. Leahy

UNIVERSITY OF NOTRE DAME PRESS
NOTRE DAME—LONDON

Copyright © 1981 by
University of Notre Dame Press
Notre Dame, Indiana 46556

Library of Congress Cataloging in Publication Data

Main entry under title:

New Directions in labor economics and industrial
  relations.

  1. Industrial relations — United States — Addresses,
essays, lectures.   2. Labor economics — Addresses, essays,
lectures.   I. Carter, Michael J.   II. Leahy, William Harrall.
HD8072.5.N48   331'.0973   81-50457
ISBN 0-268-01458-2
ISBN 0-268-01459-0 (pbk.)

Manufactured in the United States of America

Furthermore it seems unlikely that the influence of banking policy on the rate of interest will be sufficient by itself to determine an optimum rate of investment. I conceive, therefore, that a somewhat comprehensive socialization of investment will prove the only means of securing an approximation to full employment; though this need not exclude all manner of compromises and devices by which public authority will cooperate with private initiative.

J. M. Keynes, 1935
The General Theory of Employment Interest and Money

In 1929, as everyone knows, the business cycle entered into a precipitous downswing ... persons of every walk of life experienced serious — frequently tragic — curtailment of their standards of living. The effect of these changes in economic conditions upon the attitudes and group predispositions of the workers, upon the intellectual climate within which unionism operated, and upon the policy of government toward labor organization was profound.

Royal Montgomery, 1945
Organized Labor

The American economy has come a long way from the highly individualistic competitive systems described by the classical economists. Concentrated economic power is here, like it or not. The problem is somehow to develop a framework within which economic power is responsibly channeled to the public good. The hard fact is that we cannot order huge groups of workers around in a democratic society.

George Leland Bach, 1977
Economics

Contents

Contributors

Michael J. Carter is instructor in economics at the University of Utah. He previously was instructor in economics at the University of Notre Dame. He has published chapters in *The Subtle Anatomy of Capitalism* and *The Limits of Educational Reform.* He presently is at work on a labor value theoretic analysis of relative wage structures.

Charles Craypo is associate professor of economics at the University of Notre Dame. He has also taught at Michigan State University and The Pennsylvania State University and has been active in university labor education. He has published articles on the economics of collective bargaining in a variety of industries, administrative labor law and corporate consolidation and internal union decision-making. He is currently completing an introductory book on the political economy of collective bargaining.

David M. Gordon is professor of economics at the New School of Social Research. He received his Ph.D. from Harvard University and is Director of the Institute for Labor Education and Research in New York. In addition to articles on labor markets, poverty, and political economy and economic crises he has published books on *Theories of Poverty and Under-employment, Problems in Political Economy: An Urban Perspective,* and *Labor Market Segmentation.*

Charles C. Killingworth is university professor at Michigan State University. He is past president of the Industrial Relations Research Association and served as chairman of the National Wage Stabilization Board in 1952-1953. Professor Killingsworth serves as a permanent arbitrator for many national companies and unions. He has published extensively in many journals, and his most recent book is *Tax Cuts and Employment Policy in Job Creation: What Works.*

William H. Leahy is professor of economics at the University of Notre Dame. He is an arbitrator with the Federal Mediation and Conciliation Service and American Arbitration Association. The author of five previous books in the area of labor and urban-regional economics, he has written articles in such journals as *Land Economics, The Arbitration Journal, Growth and Change, Personnel Journal,* and the *Review of Social Economy,* among others.

Lester C. Thurow is professor of economics at the Massachusetts Institute of Technology. In addition to publishing widely in a variety of economic journals he has published a number of books including: *Poverty and Discrimination, Investment in Human Capital, Generating Inequality,* and *The Zero Sum Society.* He is called upon frequently to testify before Congress and to be interviewed on television. He has served on the staff of the Council of Economic Advisors and has been an economic advisor to several leading presidential candidates.

Preface

ENERGY CRISES, FISCAL CRISES, and, worst of all, inflation—this is the economic bad news currently filling newspaper front pages across the country. Why worry about labor relations and labor policy now? Aren't our economic problems due to government overspending and overmeddling; or perhaps to a societywide failure to "tighten our belts," and reduce energy consumption? Such is the wisdom conventional among many pundits of the press and economics profession.

But countries such as Japan, West Germany, and Sweden—all of which are characterized by higher degrees of government regulation of business than the U.S., and all of which import an even higher proportion of their oil than the U.S.—have managed to maintain far lower rates of unemployment than the U.S. at comparable rates of inflation (West Germany's inflation rate has actually been lower than the U.S.'s during the past ten years). Nor have they suffered the disastrously negative trade balances and currency devaluations that have plagued the U.S. This suggests that the problems of the U.S. economy are more complex than the pundits care to admit.

One undisputed (if little understood) fact is that rates of growth of labor productivity have dropped dramatically in the U.S., declining from an average 3.1 percent per annum growth rate during the 1947–70 period to an average 1.8 percent per annum growth rate since 1970. Rates of growth of GNP per worker have fallen even further, declining to .2 percent per annum since 1970. Could stagflation be a consequence of stagnation? Could we increase rates of productivity growth through redesigning employment policy? Is it merely coincidence that Japan, West Germany, and Sweden all have governments committed to maintaining low levels of unemployment, and systems of industrial relations which impose strong formal and informal constraints on firms which lay off or terminate workers?

Those willing to countenance the possibility that increased labor productivity is the key to reduction of trade deficits, to absorption of increased energy costs without reductions in real living standards, and, yes, even to reduction of inflation, should be quite interested in the analyses of Charles Killingsworth and Lester Thurow in this volume. Both authors argue that labor markets are characterized by pervasive structural rigidities which[1] (1) frustrate the efforts of conventional monetary and fiscal policies to promote high levels of aggregate demand and employment without simultaneously generating substantial inflation and (2) hold back the rate of growth of aggregate productivity. Within the framework of this common theme the essays complement one another. Killingsworth provides a historical overview of the achievements and failures of federal policies directed toward maintenance of full employment since 1950, while Thurow concentrates on the micro foundations of labor market wage-adjustment mechanisms and their relation to the phenomenon of simultaneous high unemployment and high inflation.

The labor-market rigidities which concern Killingsworth stem from the high material and psychic costs which individual workers must incur in order to relocate or retool for new occupations when their jobs disappear amidst the ceaseless technological change and organizational regrouping of capital. Faced with limited finances and limited information on available alternative opportunities, few such workers will be able to generate the funds and spirit to make a fresh start in a new community, a new career. Nor will fiscal and monetary policies aimed at stimulating aggregate demand help such workers to become productive members of society again. Long before labor markets tighten to the degree that employers are motivated to seek out and retrain those left behind by technological and organizational change, buoyant demand in product markets and bottlenecks in the expansion of fixed capital and of certain categories of highly skilled labor would combine to inflate prices to politically unacceptable levels. The resolution of this dilemma for Killingsworth lies in a renewed and vastly expanded commitment to federal manpower planning, to increased organization and subsidization of job retraining and job relocation programs. Given this perspective, he reinterprets the postwar record of trends in unemployment and labor-force participation so as to illustrate the propositions: that structural unemployment has been a growing problem throughout the postwar era, especially for those with limited formal education (and since 1970 for certain groups of highly educated labor such as academic professionals); that the vaunted success of the 1964 tax cut in reducing levels of unemployment throughout the latter half of the 60s was largely due to structural changes in the composition of employment induced by the Vietnam War and to statistical antifact; and that federal manpower programs in the last decade, contrary to conservative mythology, have been shown by methodologically careful studies to have benefit/cost ratios well in excess of 1.

Lester Thurow's essay points to an entirely different set of labor-market rigidities than those which concern Killingsworth and relates these rigidities to the intractability of inflation as well as unemployment. Thurow argues that not only are money wages inflexible downward but, moreover, the structure of relative wages is relatively inflexible. Nor is wage inflexibility merely a product of union policy or minimum-wage legislation. Rather, wage inflexibility is mandated by the social requirements of skill transmission and of work-group cooperation. Thus, employers cannot allow competition from younger, less-experienced workers to depress wages of their experienced employees or the latter will never reveal the "tricks of the trade" to the former. More generally, workers neither produce nor consume as isolated individuals but as members of social groups. Their morale and their willingness to cooperate with each other and with the general objectives of management depend on their perception that they are being treated equitably, a perception which is bound to be upset by sudden or sharp changes in the customary structure of wages. Hence employers are reluctant to reduce the wages of any type of labor simply because surpluses of that type of labor materialize. On the other hand, wage increases wrangled by a significant group of workers anywhere in the economy will generate tremendous pressure on employers throughout the system similarly to increase their employees' remuneration, even in the face of product and labor market slack.

Add mark-up pricing behavior by businesses in oligopolistic and regulated industries to this scenario, and the stage is set for the rapid transmission throughout the economy of an upward price "shock" anywhere within it. Unless the Federal Reserve wants to cut back sharply the growth of the money supply and raise interest rates—in the face of what may already be high levels of unemployment—it must fund the inflation. And thus it has come to pass that the inflation initially generated by deficit financing of military expenditures during the Vietnam War was accelerated by a series of "exogenous" price shocks in the 1970s, including mismanaged farm policy and OPEC price increases. Whenever the Federal Reserve has moved decisively to restrict monetary growth, inflation has abated but unemployment shot up to politically unacceptable levels.

What can be done? Thurow's view that rigidity of relative wages and stability of employment are necessary to maintenance of high average work-group productivity tells against simplistic proposals for fighting inflation by slashing government spending or dealing with youth unemployment by reducing minimum wages. Thurow argues that only wage subsidies to employers who hire youths can decrease youth unemployment rates without upsetting customary wage scales, while only increases in average labor productivity can lead to a deceleration of inflation without imposing real costs on labor or capital or without creating a cumbrous government bureaucracy to administer wage/price controls. Of course everyone would be happy to see an increase in productivity. The novelty of Thurow's analysis lies in his suggestion that to increase productivity we must move toward arrangements which would further *reduce* competition in labor markets. We must encourage the formation of stable work groups with employment security at their respective firms.

For some Thurow may be somewhat vague about the concrete policies which the federal government could implement to achieve this goal of increasing employment security and stability, and about how this goal can be reconciled with the need to shift labor out of declining industries and into growth areas. But even readers disappointed on this count or disagreeing with his premises may find their own views on current U.S. problems challenged by the provocative and seldom-noted statistical facts which Thurow uncovers throughout his essay. For example, gross investment in fixed plant and equipment, as a proportion of GNP, was higher overall in the stagnant 70s than in the surging 60s! Or again, despite the uproar about EPA and OSHA regulations the rates of productivity growth in manufacturing have not declined.

Whatever one may think of the analyses of Killingsworth and Thurow linking labor-market rigidities to the impotence of monetary and fiscal policies to achieve simultaneously price stability and high employment, the fact of impotence itself is abundantly clear. As Arthur Schlesinger pointed out on the fiftieth anniversary of the stock market crash of 1929:

> As the pre-New Deal economy had an inherent propensity toward depression, the post-New Deal economy has an inherent propensity toward inflation. But orthodoxy is as impotent in the face of rising prices today as it was half a century ago in face of declining output. Our masters know no more how to end inflation in 1979 than John W. Davis and W. W. Atterbury knew how to end depression in 1933. . . . It may be no more prudent now than it was fifty years ago to sell the heretics short.[2]

One of the heretical ideas embraced by Franklin Roosevelt was that encouraging the growth of trade unions and collective-bargaining mechanisms could facilitate economic recovery by simultaneously promoting increased cooperation of labor with management and expanding aggregate purchasing power. The former feature would increase productivity; the latter would permit absorption of the resultant increased flow of commodities without declines in price or profit margins.

The final two essays in this book by Charles Craypo and David Gordon analyze the postwar behavior of unions. Craypo chronicles the declining strength of unions during the past two decades across a wide variety of industries in which they were once strong. He traces this decline to technological developments which have eliminated many traditional job skills that only experienced, union workers possessed. Coupled with the increasing centralization of capital into large multiproduct, transnational firms, these developments have facilitated the adoption of hard-line antiunion tactics by management and the shift of production facilities to nonunion areas. Meanwhile, the unions have failed to develop any coherent or comprehensive strategies for coping with the erosion of their bases of bargaining power. Craypo notes that the lack in existing labor law of effective sanctions on employers who violate workers' rights in an effort to maintain a "union free" environment cripples efforts to organize in the low-wage right-to-work states to which capital is fleeing. But the weakness of existing labor law can be seen as a symptom, rather than a fundamental cause, of the general malaise of the labor movement. Craypo suggests that the law cannot be changed, and the decline in unionization halted, without attacking this malaise at its source: the isolation of organized labor from middle-class liberal sympathizers and from workers outside the traditional industrial and geographic centers of union activity. The labor movement must discard its traditional conservative focus on bread-and-butter wage issues and seek to build a majority political coalition with the strength to impose legislative restrictions and obligations on capital.

Beyond noting that "this approach means that labor will have to sympathize with and address the causes of interest to the groups it would have to join with in building a majority political coalition," Craypo does not spell out the required changes in union structure and behavior. However, the timeliness of his analysis is evidenced by the movement of some prominent unions toward socially conscious activities incompatible with traditional union focus on expanding employment and raising wages. For example, the Oil, Chemical, and Atomic Workers have spearheaded drives for tighter safety standards in chemical production and for stricter testing procedures prior to the introduction of new chemicals. Similarly, the machinists have been active in efforts to control the arms race and convert weapons production facilities to production responsive to consumer and environmental concerns.

But will the union movement as a whole rise to the challenge of the times and present as it did in the 1930s an alternative to the sometimes not-so-benevolent corporations' urgings that we all tighten our belts, accept unsafe work, unhealthy air, and declining social services in order to increase investment incentives? Or will the unions cling to traditional business unionism policies which emphasize industry profitability as a key source of union bargaining power? Those interested in thinking seriously about this issue will be challenged by David Gordon's essay on the determinants of union structure and behavior. In what is perhaps the most theoretically ambitious essay in this volume, Gordon attempts to identify the forces impinging on union leadership and rank-and-file workers that have determined their behavior.

Although the literature on the American labor movement is replete with analyses of the determinants of
union policy, Gordon argues that most prior discussions
have been ad hoc and particularistic or vitiated by a
strong normative bias toward the institutionalization of
centralized collective bargaining as a means of resolving
tensions between workers and management.

Gordon seeks to remedy these deficiencies in the literature through articulation of three tiers of determinants
of union behavior. The initial, and most abstract, tier
identifies determinants that flow from the basic structural antagonisms between labor and capital which in-
here in any production system characterized by wage
labor and competition among capitals and workers. The
next tier identifies determinants of changes over time in
the forms of union organization and in rank-and-file
activity. The final, and most concrete, tier of determinants identifies sources of variation across unions in
rank-and-file militancy and in union structure. The insights into union structure and behavior evolved at each
tier of the anlaysis inform the analysis of the more
particular historical and cross-sectional variations in
union behavior discussed in succeeding tiers. Readers
unfamiliar with this method of progressive concretiza-
tion, or with Marxist analyses of capitalist accumulation
and crises on which Gordon builds his structure of determinants, may nonetheless be intrigued by many of his
specific hypotheses, particularly in the sections of his
essay on the relationship between the structure of informal work groups and the distribution of power within
union structures. Gordon derives a variety of novel
hypotheses which readers will want to test against the
background of their own experiences and knowledge of
the history of labor organization.

However, Gordon refrains from hazarding specific

predictions about changes in the structures of labor relations, nor does he offer policy prescriptions. He believes that the world economy is in the midst of a long period of relative stagnation and decline which will eventually—as have such periods in the past—lead to major structural changes in the social and economic institutions supporting capital accumulation.[3] During this period of decline the rank and file will become more militant as living standards and job conditions throughout the economy fail to improve. Their struggles will become more political and will increasingly call into question the legitimacy of established union leadership and of capitalist control over investment and production decisions. There is no suggestion that such activity will lead to the imminent collapse of capitalism; merely that it will ultimately force capital to alter the legal and juridical structures that presently restrict union power and organizing activities. In exchange for these concessions unions will cooperate with initiatives of the state apparatus and of individual capitals to get production moving again. Gordon makes no effort to specify the terms of this renewed social contract between labor and capital precisely since he believes that these will be—and can only be—forged in the heat of rank-and-file struggles to increase their control over their working conditions and safeguard their established living standards. In a sense Gordon's essay is written, not for policymakers, but for union activists. His central message to them is that any actions which increase the size and homogeneity of informal work groups while breaking down the barriers of status culture and communication between them will lay the groundwork for a strong, unified, politicized rank-and-file movement during the coming crisis decade.

Thus the unifying theme running through the essays

in this volume is that recovery from the present period of economic stagnation requires new approaches to labor relations both at the level of the firm and in terms of government legal and regulatory policy. The remainder of the 1980s promise to be an exciting period for labor in which one way or another workers must receive increased protection against the vagaries of the business cycle and technological and geographic displacement. Whether the issue is one of increasing employment stability to enhance group learning, cooperation, and productivity or of increasing employment stability to avert bloody class warfare, the times are ripe for a new "New Deal" for labor.

Michael J. Carter

NOTES

1. Roger Kaufman, "Why the U.S. Unemployment Rate Is So High," *Challenge,* May/June 1978, pp. 40-49.
2. Arthur Schlesinger, Jr., "The Revolution That Never Was," *Wall Street Journal,* October 24, 1979.
3. The thesis that the U.S. economy is entering a prolonged period of relative stagnation is developed more fully by Gordon in: David Gordon, "Up and down the Long Roller Coaster," in *U.S. Capitalism in Crisis,* ed. B. Steinberg *et al.* (New York: Union for Radical Political Economics, 1978).

The Development of Employment Policy

Charles C. Killingsworth

For the first 150 years of our national history something called "employment policy" would have made about as much sense to most people as a "weather policy." There were always some people who were unemployed, of course, and now and then we had hard times with a lot of people unemployed. But hardly anybody thought that this was something that the national government could or should do anything about. The depth of understanding in this period is illustrated by the immortal remark of Calvin Coolidge in the late 1920s to the effect that when a great many people are unable to find jobs, unemployment results.

In this era, before the Great Depression, the conventional economic analysis began with the assumption that full employment was the normal condition of the economy. Departures from full employment—that is, business cycles—were not completely ignored, but they were regarded as temporary aberrations. The general belief was that joblessness was basically the fault of the individual, who either was lazy or was holding out for too high a wage.

Then came the 1930s. Never before in our history had such large numbers of people been unable to find jobs.

1

The historical statistics tell us that by 1933 about 25 percent of the labor force was unemployed in the United States. It was not comforting to observe that the industrialized nations all around the world were struggling with the same problem. Conventional economics had only one answer: cut wages. This remedy was widely used, but unemployment remained high.

The Contribution of Keynes

In the mid-1930s J. M. Keynes challenged the conventional analysis of unemployment and the cure for it. He argued that government policy could influence the levels of employment and unemployment by means that were much more effective than the discredited wage-cutting policy. Government *investment* — or expenditure — was the key. The Keynesian ideas met heavy opposition for some years, but those ideas were the seeds from which modern employment policy has grown. The Keynesian prescription did not seem to work very well in the 1930s, at least in the United States, because unemployment remained high. The Keynesians contended, however, that the shortcoming was not in the prescription but in the amounts of the remedy that were applied. Even though billions of dollars were being spent on public works and public employment, the Keynesians argued that even larger government expenditures were needed.

World War II ended the unemployment problem of the 1930s. By 1943 the national unemployment rate was below 2 percent — less than one-tenth what it had been ten years before. Some Keynesians argued (and a few still do) that the World War II experience showed the effects of an enormous increase in aggregate demand. It is important to note that other powerful influences were also at work. Nearly 12 million men were removed from the civilian labor force by the draft, and a large proportion of industrial production was covered by cost-plus contracts, which were often a 110 percent wage subsidy. Large numbers of women, young people, and retired workers entered or reentered the labor force, but total employment actually declined from 1943 to 1944, and again from 1944 to 1945.

Virtually all economists predicted the return of mass unemployment when World War II ended. That expectation was mainly responsible for the enactment of the Employment Act of 1946, which was the most significant recognition to that time that government had the power and the responsibility to pursue policies that would result in satisfactory levels of employment. However, the mass unemployment predictions of the later war years proved to be drastically mistaken. After a brief period of "reconversion" the country launched into a great postwar boom. Wartime shortages of many kinds of consumer durables had created both the demand for these items and the savings that could pay for them. Indeed, the money was so much more readily available than the goods in the immediate postwar years that we quickly developed a severe inflation problem. But greatly increased production slowed the inflation rate. There was another big jump in prices at the beginning of the Korean War, largely because consumers remembered the shortages of World War II and started a great wave of anticipatory buying. Wage-and-price controls were invoked, and inflation slowed to a creep.

The 1950s

For some reason unknown to me, the early 1950s is a

period which is almost completely ignored in contemporary discussions of economic policy. We had an inflation rate of about 1 percent per year and an unemployment rate of less than 3 percent. Of course we also had a war and wage-and-price controls. But the war was a small one, and I can testify from firsthand experience with the administration of the wage-and-price-control program that it was not highly restrictive.[1] More important, after the wage-and-price controls were terminated early in 1953, the low inflation and low unemployment rates showed scarcely a blip. This idyllic state continued until the onset of a mild recession late in 1953. Today, when we have excessive inflation and excessive unemployment, it seems fruitful to look back at least briefly and ask what has caused this great change in the performance of our economy in less than twenty years. The answer, unfortunately, is that so many things have changed that there is broad disagreement about which are most important and what remedial steps are suggested by such a review of the recent past.

In retrospect it seems clear that 1953–54 was a major turning point for our economy. For the purposes of this discussion the most important change was that the prosperity-period unemployment rate started to rise in a stair-step fashion. (See chart 1.) By 1955 recovery was complete from the 1953–54 recession, but the unemployment rate did not return to the 3 percent level of 1953; it fell no lower than 4 percent. There was another recession in 1958, and the rather weak recovery in 1959 left the unemployment rate above 5 percent. The next recession started in 1960, and by 1963 the unemployment rate was still hovering between 5.5 and 6 percent. For many "disadvantaged" groups—such as black workers, teenagers, and the residents of depressed areas such as the old New England textile towns—unemployment rates were substantially higher than the national average.

CHART 1

UNEMPLOYMENT RATE

JANUARY 1949 TO 1963

(SEASONALLY ADJUSTED)

PERCENT OF CIVILIAN LABOR FORCE

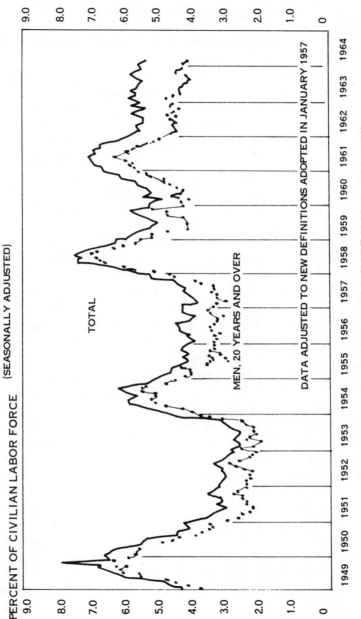

TOTAL

MEN, 20 YEARS AND OVER

BEGINNING IN JANUARY 1960, DATA INCLUDE ALASKA AND HAWAII.

DATA ADJUSTED TO NEW DEFINITIONS ADOPTED IN JANUARY 1957

Unemployment in the 1960s and 1970s

This development was called "creeping prosperity un-employment," and it was widely discussed during the 1950s. John F. Kennedy made unemployment one of the major issues of his presidential campaign in 1960, and he repeatedly promised to "get this country moving again." After Kennedy won the election, he proposed an economic stimulus program centered on a large federal tax cut. The tax cut was debated at some length and finally was enacted early in 1964. The unemployment rate remained above 5 percent until 1965, when it started dropping fairly steadily. By 1969 the rate was down to 3.5 percent. This outcome was widely regarded as strong evidence of the appropriateness of the economic policies of the early 1960s, especially the tax-cut prescription. However, when U.S. involvement in Vietnam started to wind down, the unemployment rate began to rise again.

Higher unemployment in the early 1970s at first was dismissed as a "transitional" problem by administration economists, who were apparently implying that unemployment would decrease after we had readjusted to peacetime conditions. Now, at the end of the 1970s, it seems apparent that the pre-Vietnam unemployment problem has reappeared. We apparently reached a cyclical peak sometime in the first half of 1979, when the official unemployment rate was a little below 6 percent. And, as I will explain in more detail a little later, if we applied the definitions of employment and unemployment that were followed before 1965, the official unemployment rate in the first half of 1979 would have been almost a full percentage point higher than the reported number. In other words, by pre-1965 standards unemployment was close to 7 percent in the first half of 1979.

The Policy Debate of the 1960s

Thus far this narration has given only incidental attention to the economic policy discussions that were stimulated by the ups and downs of the unemployment rate. I have mentioned the initial prescription for the cure of the mass unemployment of the 1930s—wage-cutting—and I have also mentioned the markedly different prescription of J. M. Keynes. I suggested that the mistaken prediction of the return of mass unemployment after World War II was largely responsible for the enactment of the Employment Act of 1946. Since unemployment remained at reasonably satisfactory levels (except for brief recessions) for nearly a decade after the passage of the Employment Act, there was little discussion of employment policy during these years.

The development of "creeping prosperity unemployment" in the latter half of the 1950s revived the discussion of employment policy. In the 1930s virtually all areas of the country and all groups of the population had been affected by the mass unemployment of that era. The unemployment of the late 1950s was much more concentrated. The New England states, Appalachia and other parts of the South, the heavy manufacturing centers around the Great Lakes, and a few other areas had disproportionate numbers of workers without jobs. Unemployment was disproportionately high among blacks, teen-agers, less-educated workers, blue-collar workers in manufacturing industries, and certain other groups.

Two economic policy approaches to the unemployment problems of the 1950s began to emerge. The first emphasized what came to be called the "structural" aspects of the problem. Textbooks in labor economics had long recognized the point that changes in technology, shifts in the location of industries, changes in consumer buying patterns, the exhaustion of natural resources, migration of the labor force, and so on could produce a type of unemployment which for years had been called "structural," on the basis that changes of this kind were alterations of the "structure" (or the relationships between the parts) of the economy. There was general agreement that such changes in structure were inherent in the functioning of a dynamic economy. Some economists had argued that the labor market would lead those who were displaced by structural change to other kinds of work. Others argued that the labor market might operate very slowly with regard to some groups and areas, and that the "natural" functioning of the labor market might need supplementation by government programs of special training, relocation assistance, and special inducements for new industries to locate in areas of high unemployment.[2]

The Kennedy Council of Economic Advisors (CEA) appointed in 1961 quickly rejected the view that structural changes in the economy had anything to do with the creeping prosperity unemployment of the 1950s.[3] The council did not deny that there had been significant structural changes in the economy in the 1940s and the 1950s. The council insisted, however, that its studies showed no *increase* in the volume or effects of structural change; therefore, it argued, the causes of rising prosperity unemployment had to be found elsewhere. The council's diagnosis was that the primary cause was "fiscal drag." Recovery from a recession and long-term economic growth produced rising personal and business incomes, the council pointed out, and the progressive federal income tax took an increasing share of the growing income. The growth of tax receipts outran the growth of federal expenditures, and the disparity created a "drag" on the recovery. Therefore, the council said, recoveries were aborted before the full potential of the economy had been realized. The council's main policy conclusion was that the "centerpiece" of economic policy should be a massive reduction in federal personal and business income taxes.

The council did not flatly oppose the policy approaches which were commonly called the "structural" remedies: for example, manpower retraining, relocation, area redevelopment, and the like. However, the council did argue that such measures as these would be ineffective as long as fiscal drag was allowed to impede the expansion of the economy. Therefore, the council said, priority should be given to tax-cutting and similar measures of overall economic stimulus. After the unemployment rate was reduced to the "interim target" of 4 percent, then greater emphasis could be given to structural-type remedies.

An Assessment of CEA Contentions

The preceding paragraphs represent a drastic condensation of a line of argumentation which ran to hundreds of thousands of words. Not all of these words came from the Council of Economic Advisors or other administration sources. Most reputable economists agreed with the council arguments and said so at length in many forums. And the outnumbered "structuralists," as they came to be called, answered back. I defer a summary of the main structuralist arguments in order to offer a brief critique of the council's main lines of argument. The council and its allies at first relied heavily on an econometric refutation of what the council called "the structural hypothesis." The first version of this refutation appeared under the auspices of the Joint Economic

Committee of the Congress,[4] which the council adapted.[5] Then other, mainly academic, scholars took up the attack on the structural hypothesis. Without any exception known to me, all of the studies of this kind concluded that there was little or no merit to the structural hypothesis.

The structuralists replied that the so-called "structural hypothesis" which was so strongly attacked was nothing more than a straw man. The alleged hypothesis was not based on anything said or written in the 1950s (or any other time) by anyone identified as a structuralist. The so-called structural hypothesis was nothing less than a hoax by the authors of the original Joint Economic Committee study. The unquestioning acceptance of this hoax by most of the leaders of the economics profession when its fraudulent nature could easily have been detected raises questions about the standards of scholarship in this profession.[6] In fact, published contemporary criticisms of the alleged structural hypothesis appeared in the 1960s,[7] but they were ignored by a number of academics who were still turning out refutations of this chimera.

Econometric refutations of the "structural hypothesis" straw man were convincing to most professional economists, but most were too esoteric to be easily understood by the general public (and most congressmen). In the late 1960s another simpler refutation was developed. The great tax cut advocated by the Council of Economic Advisors had been passed early in 1964. At first the unemployment rate — which then stood at 5.8 percent — showed little response. At the end of 1964 the rate was still 5 percent. In 1965, however, the rate began to fall more rapidly; by the end of the year the "interim target" of 4 percent had been achieved, and in 1966 and 1967 the rate continued to decline. By early 1969 the lowest rate of the 1960s — 3.3 percent — had been achieved. The tax-cut advocates were quick to attribute this dramatic development to the tax cut. In the late 1960s and well into the 1970s many prominent economists asserted that the behavior of the unemployment rate during the 1964–69 period was conclusive proof that the structuralists had been completely wrong in the debate of the early 1960s, and that the tax cut had proved to be even more effective than its advocates had expected. Among those advancing such arguments were four past presidents of the American Economic Association—and some future presidents as well, no doubt.[8]

Effects of 1964 Tax Cut

The hidden assumption in this analysis was that the 1964 tax cut was the only substantial factor causing the decline in the unemployment rate. This assumption was patently unrealistic. Many other factors were at work during this period, and their combined effect accounted for far more of the reduction in the unemployment rate than could conceivably be attributed to the tax cut. I will identify each of these factors only briefly, because I have discussed them at greater length in other publications.[9]

The first factor was two changes in the definitions of unemployment. One occurred early in 1965. The change was to count enrollees in certain government job-creation programs as employed. Back in the 1930s enrollees in comparable programs such as the Works Progress Administration (WPA) and National Youth Administration (NYA) had been counted as *unemployed*. (They still are in the historical statistics.) Beginning in 1965, enrollees in programs such as Neighborhood Youth Corps (NYC), College Work-Study, and On-the-Job Training (OJT) (as well as a number of smaller programs) were counted in the official labor-market statistics as *employed*. The effect was relatively small in 1965—a reduction of 0.2 percent in the reported unemployment rate—but as these programs increased in size, the effect also increased. By 1969 this definition change had resulted in a reported unemployment rate that was 0.5 percent lower than it would have been under the pre-1965 definitions.[10] The second change in definitions was made in 1967. This was actually a group of changes, such as the elimination of 14- and 15-year-olds from the labor-market statistics and the tightening of the definition of "seeking work." The Bureau of Labor Statistics estimated that the combined effect of these 1967 changes was a reduction of 0.2 percent in the reported unemployment rate.[11]

Another major factor was the military draft and some of its indirect effects. The total number of persons in the U.S. armed forces increased by about 1 million during the Vietnam War, with the expansion beginning early in 1965. Most of those taken by the draft would have been employed if they had not been drafted, so the draft opened up a large number of vacancies in civilian employment, most of which were filled by persons who would otherwise have been unemployed. The draft (and a policy of deferment for college students) also caused a sharp increase in full-time male college enrollments starting in the fall of 1965, thereby further decreasing the number of persons competing for civilian jobs. A careful estimate of the net effect of the military draft on the unemployment rate is a reduction of 0.9 percent by 1969.[12]

The effects of the definition changes and the draft can be estimated with a reasonable degree of confidence. My best judgment is that the estimates reported here are probably as accurate as most government statistics. The combined effect on the unemployment rate of these factors other than the tax cut is a reduction of 1.6 percent by 1969. In other words, in the absence of the definition changes and the draft the 1969 unemployment rate would have been 4.9 percent rather than the reported 3.3 percent. From the 5.8 percent level of early 1964 to the 3.3 percent level of early 1969 the reduction in the unemployment rate was 2.5 points. Roughly two-thirds of that reduction is properly attributable to the definition changes and the effects of the draft. (See chart 2.) What appears to be the consensus judgment of economists that the *entire* reduction is attributable to the tax cut of 1964 overstates the real effect of the tax cut by a factor of about three. This point merits emphasis because the conventional analysis of the drop in unemployment in the 1960s has remained essentially unaffected by demonstrations of the fallacies in that conventional analysis. We still hear the argument that it was "simple fiscal and monetary policy" that brought the unemployment rate down almost to 3 percent in the late 1960s.[13] This major error in the analysis of the 1960s leads to large errors in the analysis of current economic developments and policy prescriptions.

Two other points should be mentioned quite briefly. In addition to causing an increase in the size of the armed forces, the Vietnam War also caused a substantial increase in defense-related employment.[14] From 1965 to 1968 the estimated size of this increase was 1.3 million jobs. The mix of jobs thus created heavily favored less-skilled workers, who had had disproportionately high unemployment rates during the late 1950s and early 1960s. During the 1965–68 period only 15 percent of the new white-collar jobs generated by the economy were in defense employment, but nearly 50 percent of the blue-collar jobs were in defense employment. Despite this

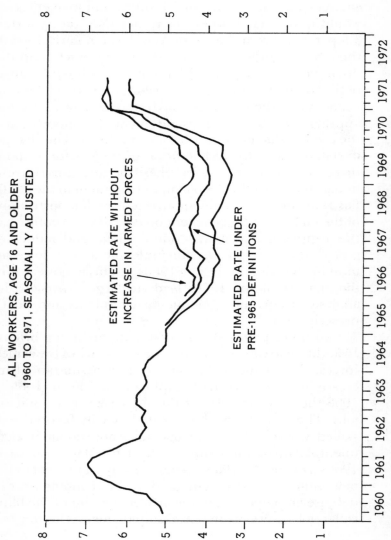

CHART 2   U.S. UNEMPLOYMENT RATE BY QUARTERS

ALL WORKERS, AGE 16 AND OLDER
1960 TO 1971, SEASONALLY ADJUSTED

ESTIMATED RATE WITHOUT
INCREASE IN ARMED FORCES

ESTIMATED RATE UNDER
PRE-1965 DEFINITIONS

temporary increase in the opportunities for less-skilled workers their labor-market position deteriorated during the 1960s. The total number of jobs held by lower-skilled and less-educated workers actually decreased, and labor-force participation rates of these groups also fell—with the sharpest drop in the rates for the least educated. This point will be further developed below.

Structural Change Examined

Thus far structural change in the economy has been discussed in general terms. Some of the specifics of structural change, and their effects, will now be more closely examined. Chart 3 shows the changing distribution of employment among certain major industry classifications during the past quarter-century. Manufacturing and agriculture have been shrinking relatively, while trade, education, and medical care have been notable among the growth industries. Chart 4 shows some of the same data in a more aggregated form. This chart reveals that the economy passed a significant milestone in 1953. In that year employment in service-producing industries first exceeded employment in goods-producing industries. The disparity has increased year by year. Goods employment is now below the level of 1953, while service employment has roughly doubled since 1953.

Chart 5 presents indexes of three important variables in agriculture for the half-century between 1920 and 1970. Several points of major significance emerge from a close examination of this chart. Clearly, agriculture has had a major technological revolution, starting in the mid-1930s and accelerating after World War II. Output per man hour in 1970 was about seven times as much as in 1950. Total output grew much less rapidly than productivity. The result was an accelerating decline in employment in agriculture. The slowly growing demand for agricultural products could be met by fewer and fewer people.

These are not facts which are presented here for the first time. They are so familiar that they are trite. But too little attention has been given to the labor-market consequences of the agriculture revolution. Farmworkers are,

CHART 3

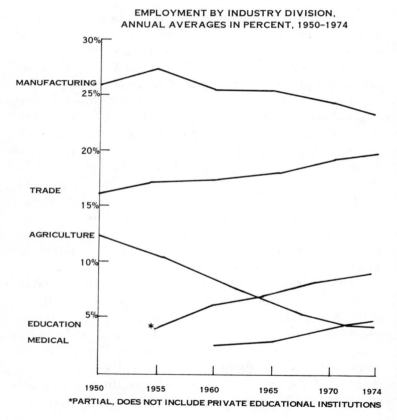

EMPLOYMENT BY INDUSTRY DIVISION,
ANNUAL AVERAGES IN PERCENT, 1950–1974

*PARTIAL, DOES NOT INCLUDE PRIVATE EDUCATIONAL INSTITUTIONS

CHART 4

MILLIONS

EMPLOYMENT IN GOODS-PRODUCING INDUSTRIES
COMPARED WITH EMPLOYMENT IN SERVICE INDUSTRIES
ANNUAL AVERAGES, 1919 TO 1976

SERVICE 2.

GOODS 1.

1. GOODS-PRODUCING INDUSTRIES
   INCLUDE AGRICULTURE, MINING,
   MANUFACTURING, AND CON-
   STRUCTION.
2. SERVICE INDUSTRIES INCLUDE
   TRADE, FINANCE, SERVICE,
   GOVERNMENT, TRANSPORTATION,
   AND PUBLIC UTILITIES.

generally speaking, the least-educated group in the labor force. In earlier years most of their work skills were learned on the job, and not much of the farmer's skills could be used in a factory or an office. Especially after World War II rapidly rising productivity on farms dis-

CHART 5

INDEXES OF PRODUCTIVITY, OUTPUT, AND EMPLOYMENT IN AGRICULTURE 1920–1970
(1920 = 100)

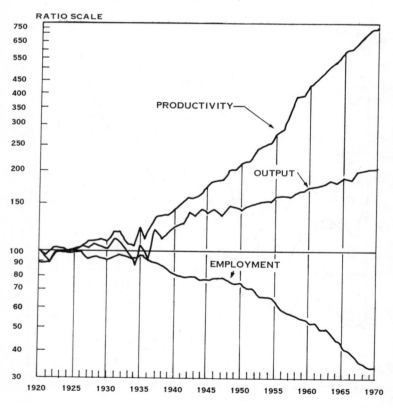

placed millions of farmworkers. They crowded into the lower strata of urban labor markets, increasing the competition for the less-skilled jobs at a time when the total number of such jobs was shrinking. Many displaced farmworkers did find jobs in factories and elsewhere. But their migration into urban labor markets clearly increased the imbalance in these markets between the kinds of skills offered and the kinds of skills required by the growth industries.

There was irregular growth in employment in manufacturing after World War II, although (as implied by chart 3) this growth was at a slower rate than the growth of the labor force. There was a significant change in the composition of employment in manufacturing. As shown by chart 6, the ratio of nonproduction (mainly white-collar) workers in manufacturing has risen fairly steadily in the postwar years. Stated differently, the share of white-collar workers in manufacturing employment has increased substantially. Back in the 1920s the white-collar share was 19 to 20 percent; this share dropped during World War II, rose steadily to about 26 percent at the beginning of the Vietnam War, dipped, and then rose further to a little more than 28 percent in 1977. War production requires large increases in the blue-collar work force in manufacturing (chart 7); this was true not only during the Vietnam War but also during World War II and the Korean War. Except for these temporary surges there has been little change in the level of employment of blue-collar workers in manufacturing since the end of World War II.

In many respects the automobile industry has been the bellwether for American manufacturing during most of the twentieth century. It is instructive to examine the growth of demand for automobiles. The left-hand panel

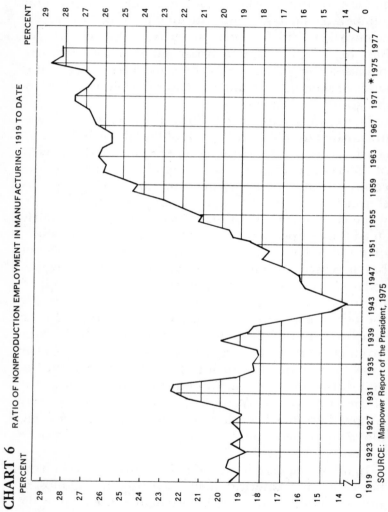

CHART 6   RATIO OF NONPRODUCTION EMPLOYMENT IN MANUFACTURING, 1919 TO DATE

SOURCE: Manpower Report of the President, 1975

*Employment & Training Report of President, Dept. of Labor & HEW, 1978, p. 263, Table C-2.

of chart 8 does so somewhat indirectly; it shows the growth of the total stock of automobiles in the U.S. during the twentieth century. In the early years the automobile population increased many times as fast as the human population. The stock of automobiles increased enormously, and the ratio of persons to cars dropped with corresponding rapidity, as shown by the right-hand panel of chart 8. After World War I the stock of automobiles doubled in about five years; after World War II the stock doubled in about 14 years; in the 1970s the growth rate has been even slower. The reason for slower growth is apparent in the ratio between persons

CHART 7

PRODUCTION WORKER EMPLOYMENT IN MANUFACTURING, 1919–1976

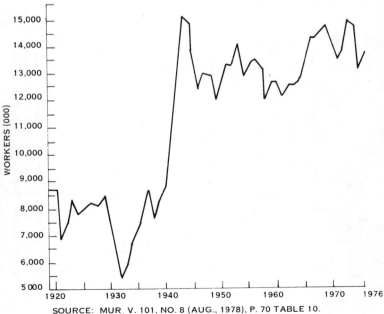

SOURCE: MLR, V. 101, NO. 8 (AUG., 1978), P. 70 TABLE 10.

CHART 8

AUTOMOBILE REGISTRATIONS AND PERSONS PER AUTOMOBILE IN
THE UNITED STATES, 1900–76

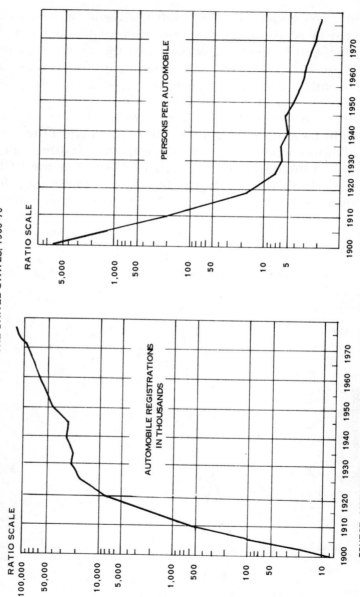

SOURCE: MOTOR VEHICLE FACTS AND FIGURES, 1978, U.S. BUREAU OF THE POPULATION CENSUS, STATISTICAL ABSTRACT
OF THE U.S.: 1977 (98TH EDITION) WASHINGTON, D.C. 1977, P. 5.

and automobiles. In 1918 we had one car for each 20 persons; in 1946, one for each 5 persons; and by 1976 we had one car for every two men, women, children, and infants in the U.S. We are probably approaching a ratio of one car for every licensed driver. Even before the recent gasoline shortage we were rapidly approaching the day when automobile sales would necessarily be limited to replacement and population growth.

The ratio of persons to automobiles can be taken as a kind of rough index of industrial development. Table 1 shows this ratio for selected countries for 1959, 1969, and 1976. The U.S. has the lowest ratio in all of these countries. But the rate of change in our ratio has slowed

Table 1

Persons Per Automobile, Nine Countries
1959, 1969, and 1976

	1959	*1969*	*1976*
United States	3.1	2.3	2.0
Canada	4.6	3.3	2.5
Sweden	6.5	3.6	2.9
France	8.0	4.3	3.3
West Germany	14.6	4.8	3.3
United Kingdom	10.4	4.7	3.9
Italy	29.3	5.9	3.6
Japan	288.9	14.8	6.2
U.S.S.R.	363.2	154.1	86.0

Source: Motor Vehicle Facts and Figures, Motor Vehicle
        Manufacturers Association of the U.S., Inc. (Detroit,
        Michigan: 1978, 1977, 1973/4, 1971, 1960).

Source: Automobile Facts and Figures, 1971 for 1969 Data

greatly. By 1976 most of the Western European nations had ratios equal to ours in the 1950s. Japan's 1976 ratio was the same as ours in the 1920s. The U.S.S.R. ratio in 1976 was equal to ours before World War I. The automobile industries of these countries were still in the rapid-growth stage that our industry experienced years ago. Most of these countries also have larger percentages of their labor force in agriculture than we have in the U.S. (the United Kingdom is the exception), but there has also been a large migration out of agriculture in all of these countries. These observations suggest that the other major industrialized nations are following the same growth patterns that we have seen in the U.S., but that the other countries are varying numbers of years behind the U.S. in their growth patterns. To the extent that the labor-market problems of the U.S. are attributable to structural changes in the economy, perhaps other industrialized nations will face similar problems in the decades ahead. There is also a possibility, of course, that the energy crisis will change patterns of development in these other countries in coming years. But the important point is that our industrial development is considerably ahead of that of other major nations. Policies that seem to work well abroad may be less successful here, and vice versa.

Structural Change and Unemployment

The preceding discussion is intended to provide illustrations of major structural changes in the U.S. economy. As already noted, there is fairly general agreement among economists that such changes have occurred and are continuing. But, generally speaking, economists have not found this kind of change particularly significant.

Most of them have made the assumption that market mechanisms will do all that is necessary to insure the movement of workers and other resources away from those industries and sectors that are declining and into expanding sectors of the economy. The process of reallocation might result in some temporary loss of work, according to this view, but this is a small price to pay for a free-market economy.

The nature of our labor-market statistics makes it impossible to measure directly the amount of unemployment which results from structural change. Obviously it is pointless to ask an unemployed worker why he or she is unemployed; the answer would probably be "because I can't find a job" or "because I lost my last job." The official statistics do record what the unemployed worker reports as his or her last job. But a displaced farmer who works for a minimum of one hour for pay in, say, a filling station is counted as an unemployed retail trade worker. Or the displaced farmer may get a job in an automobile plant, preventing a teen-ager from taking that job; the teen-ager then would probably be counted as an unemployed person with no previous work experience. The classification of unemployed workers by the occupations and industries of their last employment is one of the more misleading kinds of labor-market data.

We must seek indirect evidence of the impact of structural change on employment and unemployment. We know, for example, that the average educational attainment of farmworkers is the lowest for any occupational group. We can reasonably expect, therefore, that the massive displacement of farmworkers during the last 30 years would have an adverse impact on all poorly educated workers. Conversely, we know that—at least until recently—education, health care, and trade were among the growth sectors of the economy; and we also know that in these industries the average educational requirements are higher than in agriculture or assembly-line jobs in manufacturing. It is reasonable to expect that labor-market data on workers classified by educational attainment should show a gradually deteriorating situation for less-educated workers and a gradually improving situation for better-educated workers. And this is exactly what these data show.[15]

Chart 9 displays the relevant data for the period from 1950 to 1962 for males 18 and older.[16] One reason for comparing these two years is that the overall unemployment rate for males 18 and older was about the same in both years: around 6 percent. The right-hand bar in each panel of this chart shows the change in the unemployment rate for each group between 1950 and 1962. The unemployment rates for the groups with less than a high-school diploma were significantly higher in 1962 than in 1950; the rate for those with the high-school diploma was little changed; and the rates for those with college training were lower—much lower for those with a college degree.

In other words, in this time period there was a substantial redistribution of unemployment from the better-educated to the less-educated. And this redistribution ran in the opposite direction from what we should have expected from the changes in the relative supply of workers at the different levels of educational attainment. The supply of workers with college training increased rapidly during this period, as shown by the left-hand bars in the relevant panels; and the supply of workers with little education decreased substantially at the same time. But jobs for the college-trained increased even more rapidly than job-seekers, and reported unemployment rates went down. Jobs for the less-educated decreased more rapidly than job-seekers, and unemployment went up.

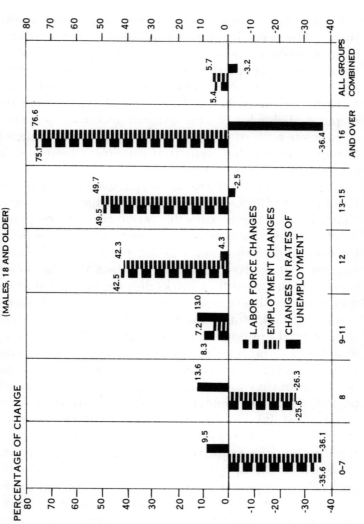

CHART 9

THE CHANGING STRUCTURE OF LABOR-FORCE
EMPLOYMENT AND UNEMPLOYMENT, 1950 TO 1962

(MALES, 18 AND OLDER)

PERCENTAGE OF CHANGE

LABOR FORCE CHANGES

EMPLOYMENT CHANGES

CHANGES IN RATES OF
UNEMPLOYMENT

YEARS OF EDUCATION COMPLETED

The Labor-Market Twist

I have called this phenomenon "the labor-market twist." The term is intended to suggest that structural changes in the economy during this period were pushing up the demand for the better-educated workers while pushing down the demand for the less-educated worker. I argued in the early 1960s, and I still believe, that this disparate behavior of employment and unemployment at opposite ends of the educational attainment scale was strong evidence that structural unemployment had increased from 1950 to 1962.

Chart 10 presents the same comparisons for the period from 1962 to 1969, with population changes added to the chart. During these years the reported unemployment rate went down substantially for the group as a whole and for each of the education classifications. Nevertheless, I suggest that analysis of the data shows that the labor-market twist was still at work, despite the fact that the outcome was different so far as reported unemployment was concerned. Note that, despite the very large expansion of total employment, the least educated classifications (0 to 7 and 8 years of education) continued to *lose* jobs at an even more rapid rate during this seven-year period than they had during the preceding twelve-year period. Their unemployment rates went down only because their labor-force participation declined more rapidly than their jobs disappeared (and also more rapidly than the population in these classifications decreased). At the upper end of the scale (persons with a high-school diploma or better) were found large increases in the respective labor-force groups but even larger increases in jobs, so that their unemployment rates also decreased. This chart illustrates how misleading it is to look only at the reported unemployment rate for a

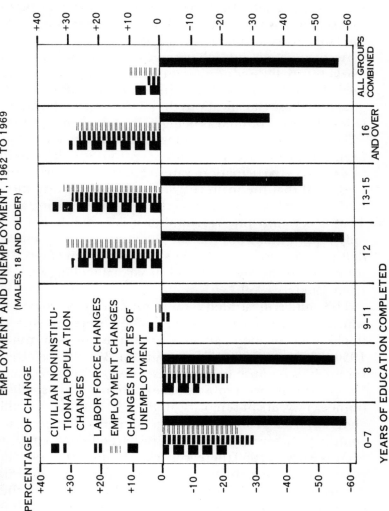

CHART 10   THE CHANGING STRUCTURE OF LABOR-FORCE
EMPLOYMENT AND UNEMPLOYMENT, 1962 TO 1969
(MALES, 18 AND OLDER)

PERCENTAGE OF CHANGE

CIVILIAN NONINSTITU-
TIONAL POPULATION
CHANGES

LABOR FORCE CHANGES

EMPLOYMENT CHANGES

CHANGES IN RATES OF
UNEMPLOYMENT

YEARS OF EDUCATION COMPLETED

0-7   8   9-11   12   13-15   16 AND OVER   ALL GROUPS COMBINED particular segment of the labor force. An unemployment rate which is falling may indicate that the labor force in that segment is decreasing more rapidly than the segment is losing jobs, or it may indicate that the hiring of that segment is running ahead of increases in the size of the labor force in that segment.

As just noted, the labor-force participation rate of workers with little education was falling during the entire period from 1950 to 1969. In somewhat simpler language, in these classifications the percentage of the population that was counted as being in the labor force (either working or looking for work) was decreasing. There has been some controversy about the reasons for changes in labor-force participation rates. Some observers have suggested that the main reason for falling participation rates among less-educated men has been advancing age. That is certainly one reason, but it is certainly not the only reason and not even the main reason. The fact is that participation rates for less-educated men showed a pronounced downward trend at virtually all age levels from 1950 to 1969.

The point is illustrated rather dramatically by chart 11, which shows labor-force participation rates by educational level for men age 35–44 at three points in time: 1950, 1962, and 1969. This age group, 35–44, is selected for analysis because most of these men are married and "settled down," with substantial experience and usually a number of.years of seniority on the job; but they are still generally free from the chronic ailments that tend to come in the later years of life. This chart tells us, first, that even as early as 1950 there were significant differences in participation rates related to education in this age group. Almost 99 percent of the college graduates were in the labor force; only 92 percent of those with less than 5 years of education were labor-force participants in 1950.

By 1969 the differences in labor-force participation at the various educational levels had increased greatly. College graduates had increased their participation slightly (to a little *above* 99 percent!), while the least-

CHART 11

CIVILIAN LABOR-FORCE PARTICIPATION RATES
MALES, AGE 35–44: 1950, 1962, 1969

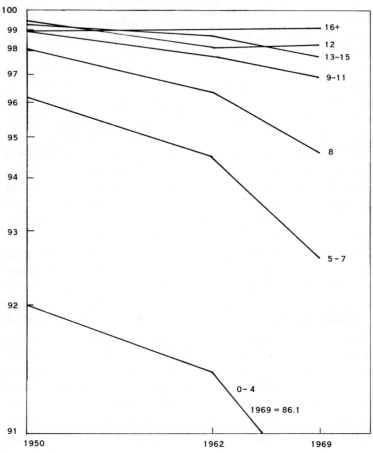

educated classification had dropped from a 92 percent rate to an 86.1 percent rate. The other educational classifications were distributed in between these two extremes.

Economic Growth and the Labor-Market Twist

It is important to note that the period from 1962 to 1969 was a time of rapid economic growth in the U.S., with the total number of jobs increasing greatly. Yet the participation rates of all the classifications with less than 12 years of education fell more rapidly *after* 1962 than before. These declines in this age group cannot logically be attributed to more generous early retirement arrangements and probably not to greater availability of disability payments. In my judgment this contrasting behavior of labor-force participation rates by education among this 35–44 age group strongly confirms the thesis that the labor-market twist was operative at least from 1950 and that it gathered strength after 1962. Or, to put the matter in more familiar terms, even the men in this "prime" age group were becoming less and less employable if their educational backround was deficient. Even at ages 35–44 they were being pushed out of the labor market. And of course the situation was worse for younger and older men with deficient education.

Some observers have suggested that the deteriorating labor-market position of less-educated workers was nothing more than a kind of mechanical result of the greater availability of better-educated workers. Employers merely have a kind of esthetic preference for those with the more impressive educational credentials: given a choice, they will hire the high-school or college graduate rather than the elementary school dropout, even though the latter might be able to meet the requirements of the job. No doubt this kind of hiring happens at times. But economic theory and common observation tell us that employers also judge the desirability of employees by what they have to pay them. If a high-school graduate and a person with five years of education were competing for the same job and if both would take the same pay rate, then usually the better-educated applicant would get the job. But if the better-educated workers were simply displacing the less-educated, with no change in the pay scales or duties of the jobs involved, then it would seem that the relative earnings of the better-educated workers would show a tendency to drop. In fact, the opposite trend is shown by the relevant data.

Education and Income

Chart 12 shows relative median annual incomes for men 25 and older by educational attainment for 1949, 1959, 1966, and 1969.[17] In the earliest year there were large earnings differentials associated with different levels of educational attainment. The male college graduate (shown as 100 on the chart) had an income in 1949 which was about two and one-half times the income of the man with less than eight years of education. With the passage of years that differential widened. By 1969 the average college graduate was earning more than three times as much as the man with less than eight years of schooling. As the chart shows, other differentials widened as well. In other words, the earnings of the college graduate relative to all other groups increased steadily. This increase in relative earnings took place during a period in which the supply of college graduates in the labor force greatly *increased,* and the supply of

CHART 12

RELATIVE MEDIAN INCOMES, MEN 25 YEARS OF AGE AND OLDER, BY EDUCATIONAL ATTAINMENT: 1949, 1959, 1966 AND 1969

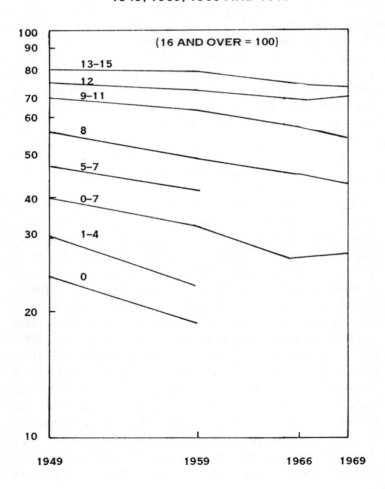

less-educated men in the labor force greatly *decreased.* Perhaps it should also be pointed out that the slope of the lines on the chart shows that the earnings of the high-school graduate improved relative to the high-school dropout, improved even more relative to the man with eight years of schooling, and so on down the line. The better-educated workers did not become less costly, nor did their cost even remain unchanged relative to less-educated workers. The better-educated workers became more costly.

These changes in relative incomes appear to provide strong confirmation for what was said above about the operation of supply-and-demand forces in the labor market during this period. Elementary economic theory tells us that a wage rate (and we may take income as the rough equivalent of a wage rate) should fall when the quantity of a particular grade of labor increases if the demand for this grade of labor is unchanged; only if the demand runs ahead of the increase of supply would we expect the wage rate to increase. The continuing rise in the relative incomes of male college graduates over the entire period from 1950 to 1969, while the numbers of such workers increased greatly, tells us that the demand for male college graduates was very strong indeed during this time. The situation was reversed in the lower strata of the labor market. The supply of males with less than a high-school diploma decreased greatly during the 1950 to 1969 period. If demand had remained unchanged, wage rates for this grade of labor should have increased. Instead, of course, the relative earnings in this sector of the labor market declined, showing that demand was decreasing even more rapidly than the supply of this grade of labor.

What emerges, it seems to me, is a picture of a split-level labor market. At the upper end, jobs seek workers

during the 1950 to 1969 period. Although the supply of
such workers is increasing rapidly, jobs are increasing
more rapidly. The strong demand for these workers
pulls up wage rates and labor-force participation rates,
and it pushes down unemployment rates in this sector of
the labor market. In roughly the bottom third of the
labor market the supply of workers is decreasing rapidly,
but the employment of these workers is decreasing even
more rapidly. The shrinking demand for such workers
pulls down relative wage rates and labor-force participation rates. It seems paradoxical that the unemployment
rates for this group should also decrease, but the decrease is entirely attributable to the fact that both the size
of the population and the size of the labor force are
shrinking even more rapidly than the number of jobs.

Recent Structural Change

No one has discovered any natural law which requires
the patterns of structural change in the economy to
remain constant or to repeat themselves. There is some
evidence that these patterns have been changing during
the 1970s. The decline of agricultural employment has
slowed, partly because productivity improvement has
slowed down and partly because the farm labor force —
after many years of almost constant shrinkage — seems to
be approaching some lower limit. The composition of the
total labor force has changed, as increasing numbers of
women and teen-agers have entered the labor market.
And the demand for college-trained workers, which was
so strong for so many years during the 1950s and the
1960s, seems to have slackened during the 1970s.
Relatively little attention has been given to the causes
for this slackening, although the fact of slackening has

been very well publicized. A quick glance at my book-shelves brings to my eyes titles like the following: *The Great Training Robbery, The Overeducated American, The Declining Value of a College Education,* and many others. The facts are reasonably clear. The college graduates of the 1970s have had greater difficulty in finding jobs than their siblings or parents did during the 1950s and 1960s. The unemployment rate for college graduates tells an important part of the story. As chart 13 shows, the unemployment rate for all (male and female) college graduates fell below 1 percent during the late 1960s. There was a rather sharp turning point in 1970, when the rate jumped to almost twice that it had been in 1969. And then the rate continued to rise (except, oddly, during 1973 and 1974), and by 1977 it was about three and one-half times what it had been in 1969. The national unemployment rate (for the entire labor force) rose from 3.5 percent in 1969 to 7 percent in 1977—that is, it doubled.

The numbers are clear enough. The causation is somewhat less clear. Some discussions seem to suggest that a cloudy abstraction called "the market" has simply undergone a change of taste: "it" no longer finds the well-educated workers as desirable as it once did. There is also some reliance on what might be called the Coolidge tautology: Since more college graduates are now unemployed, we must have produced too many of them. Actually, the numbers—which are rather startling—provide some measure of support for this general conclusion. From 1959 to 1977 the total civilian labor force increased by 25 percent; the college graduate labor force, by 67 percent. In the eight years from 1969 to 1977 the number of college graduates increased by 6.5 million persons. These numbers are part of the story, but they are certainly not the whole story.

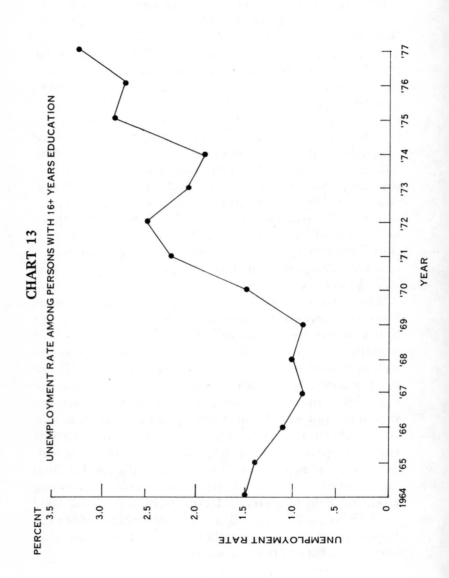

CHART 13

UNEMPLOYMENT RATE AMONG PERSONS WITH 16+ YEARS EDUCATION

Probably the single most important development affecting the college graduate labor force in the 1970s was a slowdown in the growth of employment in education. This slowdown was partly the result of demographic factors. Enrollments in elementary and secondary schools leveled off and in some communities actually declined. In addition, at the college and university level some fields (like physics) which had been heavily dependent on federal research funds found that those funds suddenly slowed to a trickle or vanished altogether. Research and development spending in private industry also decreased. It is very difficult to find figures on the flows of new college graduates into various fields of employment. Fortunately Michigan State University has made a major effort to follow its graduates and to keep records on what jobs they hold (among other things). Chart 14 shows the percentages of MSU graduates going into the education industry from 1964 to 1978. In the earlier year, as the chart shows, 55 percent of the graduates found their first job in education. By 1978 that percentage had dropped to 26 percent. There is no reason to believe that the experience of MSU graduates in the job market was unusual.[18] If we generalize that experience, we can conclude that the education industry generally was taking a sharply decreasing share of new graduates over the years. Those who did not find jobs in education obviously had to look for work in other industries, thus increasing the competition for starting level jobs in those other industries. According to anecdotal evidence some graduates are now taking blue-collar jobs which their siblings would have scorned a decade ago. And since a college degree no longer appears to be a ticket to a well-paid white-collar job, the growth in college enrollments has slowed; indeed, in some institutions the enrollment figures are actually decreasing. This development in turn has almost eliminated the market for new Ph.D.'s in some fields.

Some concluding generalizations concerning structural change in the economy appear to be in order. Perhaps the least controversial observation is that such change is an inherent and pervasive aspect of an evolving economic system. Some aspects, such as those resulting from demographic factors like a decrease in the number of school-age children, are predictable; but others, such as the sudden cutback in federal support for research in some scientific fields, are obviously not predictable. Structural change has an uneven impact among indus-

CHART 14

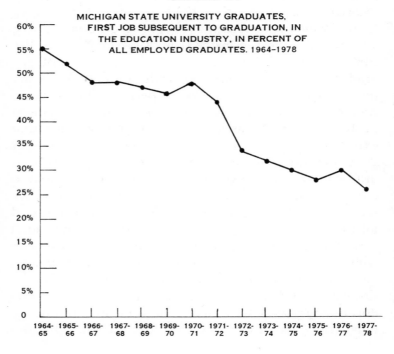

MICHIGAN STATE UNIVERSITY GRADUATES, FIRST JOB SUBSEQUENT TO GRADUATION, IN THE EDUCATION INDUSTRY, IN PERCENT OF ALL EMPLOYED GRADUATES. 1964–1978

tries, and its rate varies over time even within a single industry, such as agriculture. Structural change can greatly benefit for many years a particular group in the labor force, such as college graduates, and then almost overnight become unfavorable for this group. As this is written (mid–1979), it seems likely that the energy crisis will have major effects on the future growth patterns of the economy. Since the energy policy of the government is still largely undefined, there is little basis even for speculation about the specific effects of the end of the age of cheap energy. But the certainty of large impending changes, even though their details are still unknown, increases the relevance of an examination of the programs that we have developed to deal with the employment effects of structural change.

The Legislative Response

The growth of concern during the 1950s about structural unemployment was discussed many pages back. This concern stimulated legislative action early in the 1960s. The Area Redevelopment Act (ARA), passed in 1961, provided a wide array of assistance to distressed areas. Retraining for unemployed workers was one of the several programs under this legislation. The ARA had a small appropriation and spread it over too many areas to have a significant impact anywhere. Next came the Manpower Development and Training Act of 1962. This legislation provided for a larger program with longer training, broader eligibility, and more generous allowances for trainees than under the ARA. Both institutional and on-the-job training were provided. The appropriations under this act rose from about $70 million in FY 1963 to $130 million in FY 1964 and from about $400 million in FY 1965 to $435 million in FY 1965. Then the trend of appropriations turned down — partly because of the new War on Poverty legislation and partly because of the strain on the federal purse from the Vietnam War. The War on Poverty included some programs, such as the Neighborhood Youth Corps, that could be classified as manpower programs. For a time during the mid-1960s there was lively competition in the activity of starting new programs. There was a proliferation of activities and alphabetical identities: NYC, JOBS, WIN, CEP, JOP, PEP, PSE, PSC, and so on and on. There was not only competition for appropriations; there was competition for clients, for sponsors, for press attention, and so on. There was some duplication of effort, some launching of poorly designed and poorly administered programs, considerable public confusion, and a rising tide of criticism which condemned the whole category of "manpower programs" because of the weaknesses and failings of some.

In 1973 Congress undertook to deal with what many observers saw as the two most significant sources of weakness in manpower programs. The first was excessive categorization, meaning too many separate programs, most with their own enabling legislation, separate appropriations, separate eligibility standards, and so on. The second was excessive centralization, meaning too much control over program operations by federal authorities. Congress undertook to remedy these perceived problems by the passage of the Comprehensive Employment and Training Act (CETA) of 1973. The dominant theme of this enactment was "decategorization and decentralization."

Neither of these objectives was fully realized. Some categorical programs were carried over intact and placed under the CETA umbrella, although this was the exception rather than the rule. And a considerable measure of federal control was maintained, not only to prevent stealing but also to enforce certain eligibility and program standards. CETA represented a reorganization and a redefinition of relationships rather than an entirely new program or set of programs. However, rising unemployment in 1974 prompted a new emphasis on Public Service Employment (PSE), and the legislation covering a large-scale countercyclical PSE program became Title VI of CETA. More recently, in 1977, Congress passed the Youth Employment and Demonstration Projects Act; among other things this legislation provides for substantial youth employment programs.

The Evaluation of Manpower Programs

From their beginnings in the early 1960s the manpower programs have been studied and evaluated to an extent which is unusual if not unique among government programs. Some of the studies have been "in-house" in nature, meaning that employees of the agency administering the program under study have undertaken the research. Most of the studies, however, have been made by independent scholars. Many of these received financial support from the agency administering the program. One of the reasons for the heavy emphasis on evaluation of the manpower programs is that the techniques of "cost-benefit" analysis were being developed at roughly the same time as these programs. Therefore, the availability of money, techniques, technicians, and data converged to produce a huge volume of studies.

The outcome is paradoxical. Virtually without exception, the individual studies have concluded that manpower training in particular "pays off," in the sense that monetary benefits to the participants and to society in general exceed—sometimes by large multiples—the direct and indirect costs of such programs.[19] Only one substantial study reached a contrary conclusion, and a detailed critique of this study demonstrated that it employed what was essentially an indefensible methodology.[20] Despite the virtual unanimity of the individual studies to the effect that manpower programs in general pay off handsomely, a number of critics have reached the opposite conclusion. These critics have attacked the methodology of all of the studies and have concluded that the studies fail to establish beyond a reasonable doubt that their findings are valid. The critics then seem to apply what might be called a presumption of failure: If the evidence does not establish the success of the programs beyond a reasonable doubt, then the conclusion must be that the programs have been unsuccessful. A few other critics have painted with a broader brush. These critics say that the purpose of the manpower programs has been to reduce or eliminate excessive unemployment; since we still have excessive unemployment, it should be clear that the programs have failed.

There is a temptation to dismiss criticisms such as these with the assertion that they fall of their own weight. Perhaps that is not entirely self-evident. Perhaps it is desirable to be more specific. But some general observations are needed to provide a framework for what follows. It is important to understand that manpower programs in the United States operate in a basically hostile environment. We have a national commitment to a free-market economy. (Perhaps this commitment is stronger on the part of our political and intellectual leaders than among the general public.) During the past fifteen years or so it has also become stylish in some intellectual circles to proclaim and illustrate the idea that "government programs don't work." Since manpower programs represent a form of intervention in the labor market, and since government directs and pays for them, they are a natural target for those who hold the foregoing beliefs.

It is also necessary to concede that there are methodological problems with the evaluations of individual manpower programs. Some are no more than simple before-and-after comparisons of employment and earnings of participants, without any allowance for the independent effects of generally rising wage levels, changes in the national unemployment rate, and the effects of maturation of the participants. More sophisticated studies rely on control groups—that is, groups which are supposed to be comparable in all significant respects with the "treatment group," or the ones that get the training or experience. It is almost always possible to raise questions (or, as I have called them, "maybes") about the comparability of the control group. There are also difficult questions about such matters as discount rates and the longevity of benefits from training or work experience.

These problems raise a hard question: What is a proper standard of proof? This question is certainly not unique to manpower programs. The tobacco industry continues to insist that there is no clear proof that smoking can cause cancer, but most informed persons believe that the link has been demonstrated with reasonable certainty. Those who accepted the clearly fallacious view that all of the decline in unemployment after 1964 was due to the tax cut were surely applying an unacceptably lax standard of proof, but some of the same individuals are among those who now demand complete certainty from manpower evaluations. In my judgment these evaluations—despite all of the "maybes" that ingenuity can devise — provide substantial evidence that manpower programs generally are a good investment even from the strictly pecuniary standpoint. Actually there are wide variations in methodology, and there are large differences in the programs and participants that are evaluated; hence, it is all the more impressive that the results of the studies are almost unanimously positive.

Some manpower programs are (not surprisingly) more effective than others. Analysis has revealed some more-or-less obvious determinants of success. The more disadvantaged the participants, the lower the probability of substantial improvement in their employability and earning capacity. A training program keyed to known job vacancies is more likely to be successful than one based on the vague hope that suitable jobs can be found after training. Those who complete training programs have a better chance at jobs if the economy is expanding than if we are in a recession. These are considerations that must be taken into account both in program design and in program evaluation.

Public Service Employment

Public Service Employment is so different from manpower training that it must be given separate attention. During the 1930s there was heavy reliance on direct job creation by the federal government as a form of relief from unemployment. With minor exceptions the new manpower programs of the 1960s did not include direct job creation. This component was not added until 1971, and it was not large until 1975. At first PSE seemed to be quite favorably regarded both by politicians and by the general public. There seemed to be widespread acceptance of the value judgment that it is better to pay people for working than to pay them for not working. But within a relatively brief time the critics of PSE developed so many lines of attack that this kind of program seemed to be imperiled. In my judgment there was little merit in most of the criticisms, but they convinced many people.

It is not possible to deal with the PSE criticisms both adequately and briefly. But some of the leading criticisms should at least be summarized and assessed. One popular criticism derives from the fact that under CETA practically all of the planning and administration of PSE projects is handled by state and local governments (especially the latter). The charge is that these local units spend the federal PSE funds on people and projects that the local units would have paid for themselves in the absence of the federal program. This is called fiscal substitution. Some economists developed estimates that purported to show that substitution would be as high as 58 percent after one year and 100 percent after one and one-half years.[21] These estimates were derived from an econometric model in which, to an unusual degree, the results depended on unverifiable assumptions of the authors; and substituting equally reasonable assumptions would yield drastically different estimates of fiscal substitution.[22] A careful study based on field monitoring of the administration of PSE programs reached quite different conclusions concerning substitution. This field study estimated substitution at 15 percent in December 1977. In local units of government the rate was estimated to be 19 percent, and the estimate for nongovernment agencies that were operating projects with PSE funding was 10 percent.[23]

Even where there is substitution, it is incorrect to imply—as some critics have—that the federal funds are somehow "lost." The Congressional Budget Office has estimated that when substitution occurs, the effect is the same as if the federal funds had been disbursed under the general revenue-sharing program. Under this assumption virtually all of the funds are considered used for the purchase of goods and services by the local unit rather than for tax relief for local taxpayers or increases in state and local unit fund balances. Hence, even when substitution occurs, PSE money creates jobs.[24]

Another line of criticism is that only "make-work" jobs have been or will be created by the PSE program. Indeed, some prominent critics would define a "real" job simply as one that is created in the private sector. Unquestionably some PSE projects have involved activities of questionable value. Overall, however, the available studies appear to indicate that most participants have been performing useful work. One should keep in mind the precedent of the WPA. During the 1930s many politicians and journalists labored to create the impression that the two principal activities of WPA workers were raking leaves and leaning on shovels. Yet, to the surprise of many people, the historical record shows that WPA workers built thousands of buildings, tens of thousands of miles of highways and sidewalks, and many other physical structures which are still in use. PSE jobs appear to involve much less work on structures, but large numbers of them are in activities such as police and fire services, sanitation, health care, services for the elderly, education, and parks and recreation. Recruitment, retention, and rational planning for the constructive use of PSE workers have unquestionably been considerably hampered by stop-go financing provided by Congress.

Finally, and most recently, charges of fraud and abuse in the PSE program have appeared in volume. At least some of the inspiration for these charges comes from a recent article in a popular magazine which has frequently attacked social programs in the past. It would be amazing if there were no fraud and abuse in the PSE program. In line with the decentralization mandate of CETA, the PSE program is administered largely at the state and especially the local level, and as any reader of the daily press knows, there are some corrupt city and town governments, and even state governments are not wholly immune from corruption. When federal funds are turned over to corrupt local officials, it would be most surprising if none of the funds were stolen. When most of a city's employees acquire their jobs through political influence, we should expect the same selection criteria to apply in the filling of PSE jobs. In my opinion the great majority of state, city, and town governments are reasonably well-administered, and corruption is serious in only a minute percentage of them. Similarly, verified instances of fraud in PSE programs involve an extremely small percentage of total expenditures. Of course, it is not difficult to create the impression that a program is riddled with corruption or abuse by reciting anecdotal evidence about a dozen projects (out of thousands) or a few hundred employees (out of hundreds of thousands).

It is important to keep this kind of problem in perspective (although the critics seem determined to prevent just that). Private industry, by various estimates, loses billions of dollars in cash and goods each year to thieving employees. A few hospitals, clinics, and practitioners have defrauded the Medicare and Medicaid programs of millions (perhaps billions) of dollars. By highly selective reporting, some media writers have created the impression that alleged fraud and abuse in the CETA programs (especially PSE) greatly exceed that in any other government program of comparable size. No evidence worthy of consideration has been offered to support this impression. Nevertheless, some congressmen who have previously been friendly to the CETA program have

become highly alarmed by the charges, which their con-
stituents are now repeating to each other and to the
congressmen. Perhaps I have excessive confidence in the
common sense of congressmen and the general public,
but I am unwilling to believe that this latest line of attack,
damaging though it seems to be as this is written, will
prove to be fatal to CETA.

PSE: The Positive Aspects

Assuming that Public Service Employment will survive
in some form as an instrument of employment policy, we
may now appropriately consider some of the positive
effects of this instrument. In particular it is important to
direct attention to the macroeconomic potential. Since
the early 1960s a tendency has developed in discussions
of employment policy to treat "tax cuts" and "fiscal
policy" as synonyms. But hardly any careful analysis has
been undertaken to measure the job-creating effects of
tax cuts. Curiously, some of those who are most critical of
the alleged shortcomings of manpower-training evaluations simply presume that tax cuts are highly effective in
raising employment levels, or they accept as conclusive
evidence the fallacious analysis of the 1960s which was
discussed above. One important exception to the foregoing is a study undertaken in 1975 by the Congressional
Budget Office. This study compared four different
"Temporary Measures to Stimulate Employment."[25]
The CBO study utilized one of the standard computer-
based models of the economy to trace through the job-
creating effects of four of these measures. The CBO
conclusions imply that the gross cost per job created by a
tax cut as of 1975 was about $25,000, and the gross cost
for a PSE job was about $8,000.[26] Net costs can be

calculated by deducting from the gross costs the estimated value of unemployment compensation and welfare payments and the taxes paid by the newly employed
individuals. The result of this calculation is a net cost of
about $19,000 per job created by a tax cut and about
$3,500 per job created by PSE.

Since this difference is so large and so significant, it is
important to understand the main reasons for it. Table 2
is intended to be helpful in making the necessary comparisons.[27] The left-hand column shows (in highly sim-
plified form) the effects of a tax cut of $8 billion. In the
first round the government simply mails checks to a
number of taxpayers (or reduces the amounts withheld
from their paychecks, or in some other way leaves them
financially better off than they would have been without
the tax cut). This first-round transaction by itself does
not create any jobs. It simply leaves the U.S. Treasury
with less money and the taxpayers with more money than
they would have had without the tax cut. Only when the
taxpayers spend part of these funds is there any job
creation. And that job creation is held down by a variety
of slippages. In the first place, some of the taxpayers may
simply save all or part of the tax refund or use it to pay off
debts. Some of the stores where the taxpayers spend the
refund may meet the increased demand for their goods
out of inventories without ordering replacements; factories may expand production by increasing the work
week instead of hiring new employees; some of the goods
bought by taxpayers with refund money may be im-
ported; and so on.

The right-hand column of table 2 shows the effects of
starting up a PSE program with a budget of $8 billion for
wage payment. In the first round the government com-
mits itself to pay annual wages of $8,000 each to 1 million
workers, who in turn commit themselves to perform

Table 2

Comparison of Job Creation by Tax Cut and by Public Service

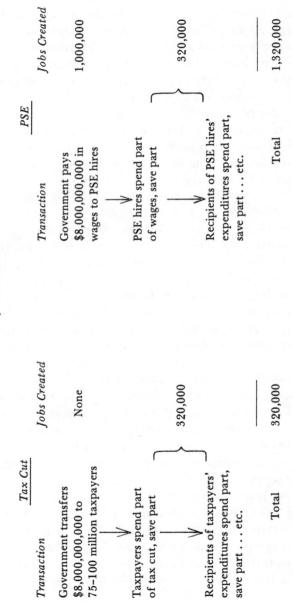

Tax Cut		PSE	
Transaction	*Jobs Created*	*Transaction*	*Jobs Created*
Government transfers $8,000,000,000 to 75–100 million taxpayers	None	Government pays $8,000,000,000 in wages to PSE hires	1,000,000
Taxpayers spend part of tax cut, save part		PSE hires spend part of wages, save part	
Recipients of taxpayers' expenditures spend part, save part . . . etc.	320,000	Recipients of PSE hires' expenditures spend part, save part . . . etc.	320,000
Total	320,000	Total	1,320,000

services during the year. In slightly simpler language, 1,000,000 jobs are created in the first round of PSE expenditure as compared with none in the first round of tax cut. This is the largest source of difference in effects. It may be perfectly obvious when it is explained, but it has almost completely been ignored in employment policy discussions. Returning to table 2, the new PSE jobholders are assumed to behave exactly like the taxpayers when it comes to spending their paychecks; they will save some and spend some, and what they spend will be subject to the same slippages as the spending of taxpayers, so far as job creation is concerned. In other words, the spending of $8 billion worth of paychecks by PSE workers will create the same number of jobs as the spending of $8 billion worth of tax refund checks by taxpayers. But the large job-creation effect in the *first* round of the PSE approach, versus zero job creation in the first round of the tax-cut approach, yields the result that the total job creation by means of PSE is four times as large as the total job creation by means of a tax cut involving the same number of dollars.

PSE and the Private Sector

Some discussions of employment policy contend that tax cuts are much more desirable than a PSE program because tax cuts create jobs in the private sector and the PSE program creates them in the public sector; it is usually taken for granted that the private-sector jobs, since they are "real," are more desirable. Such an argument ignores the important fact that, dollar for dollar, the PSE program will create just as many jobs *in the private sector* as the tax cut does. Even a high rate of fiscal substitution in the PSE program would not change this conclusion. There would be fewer jobs in the public sector, but just as many in the private sector, even with a 40 percent rate of substitution.[28]

There is still another important difference between the tax cut and the PSE instrument. Some of the characteristics of the tax-refund recipients can be specified, but the distribution of the jobs created by the spending of the tax refunds cannot be determined by public policy decisions. However, the PSE jobs can be "targeted"—which means that eligibility requirements such as length of prior unemployment, geographical location, family income, and so on can be established by policy.

This discussion is not intended to leave the impression that PSE is the ultimate solution for unemployment and that it has no real problems. The most important question about PSE is What next? Current legislation attempts to answer that question by limiting the length of time that any individual may participate. Turnover is compulsory. There are also provisions which encourage local governmental units to attempt to place PSE participants in permanent jobs on municipal payrolls. Sometimes PSE employment is combined with training for private-sector jobs. There is some evidence that a successful experience on a PSE job, plus the acquisition of letters of recommendation, improve the employability of some persons. For a great many individuals, however, a PSE job is only a stopgap which leaves unsolved the basic problem of how to earn a living over the long run. Until recently, "economic growth" was the answer usually given to this basic question. The end of cheap energy raises questions about the validity of this answer—unless, of course, we undertake multibillion dollar projects to develop sources of synthetic fuels.

A number of other approaches to the alleviation of the unemployment problem deserve more attention than it is possible to give them here. Tax incentives or direct subsidies for employers to hire disadvantaged workers are one example. Mobility assistance—loans or grants to facilitate relocation—is another example. A number of new kinds of approaches are currently being tested under the recently passed Youth Employment and Demonstration Projects Act; they are still too new to permit confident evaluation. These approaches have been tried out on a limited basis several times in the past with mixed results. Probably the safest generalization is that programs of these kinds can, under the proper circumstances, help to improve the employability of a limited number of people.

Conclusion

After many years of controversy, economists working on the unemployment problem appear to be closer to general agreement on broad lines of policy than ever before. Not all of them have followed the same route to the area of agreement. Some still would argue that tax cuts are the simplest way, and the way that is most compatible with a free-market economy, to achieve full employment; but most of them now recognize that general stimulation of aggregate demand is likely to be incompatible with inflation control. Some are even saying that structural unemployment is the most significant and the most difficult part of the overall unemployment problem. There is still some disagreement about what the particular sources of structural unemployment are, with some analysts emphasizing demographic changes such as increased proportions of women and teen-agers in the labor force. There also is still disagreement about which programs are likely to be most effective. There appears to be a lessening of the tendency to prescribe "one best" cure for unemployment and a recognition that the most effective approach is one which employs many different instruments of employment policy. There is also fairly general acceptance of the need for further experimentation and for more thorough evaluations of programs, especially those involving long-run follow-up studies of the labor-market fortunes of participants.

Many political figures seem still to be in the thrall of the conventional economic wisdom of the 1960s. When recession looms, as in mid-1979, there is much talk of tax-cutting. The talk generally concerns when and how much to cut taxes, with little or no consideration of the effectiveness of this approach compared with alternative instruments of employment policy. I do not suggest that no progress has been made in the political and legislative arena. In 1964, when Congress enacted a tax cut estimated to be worth about $13 billion, the appropriation for activities under the Manpower Development and Training Act was $130 million—a ratio of a hundred to one. In 1978, when Congress debated a tax cut of the magnitude of $15–20 billion, manpower-program expenditures were running at an annual rate of about $12 billion.

It is important to emphasize, finally, the stakes in the fight against unemployment. The point is surely not to add a few more percentage points to our national growth rate or a few more billions to our Gross National Product. The real meaning of this fight is best suggested by certain relationships which have been brought to light by recent research.[29] When the national unemployment rate goes up, then—usually with a time lag—certain other indicators also rise:

the rate of new incarcerations in state prisons,

the rate of new admissions in state mental hospitals,
the suicide rate among middle-aged men,
the death rate from strokes and heart attacks, and
the murder rate.

Nobody claims that we would all live forever and that
there would be no more unhappiness and suffering in
the land if only we solved the unemployment problem. I
say that eliminating the excessive unemployment that we
have had in this country for the past 25 years would
provide opportunities for millions of human beings to
live more fulfilling lives. We could achieve a healthier,
safer, more rewarding life for all of us — not just the least
fortunate — if we solved the unemployment problem.
When I began the study of economics, this country had
an unemployment rate of 25 percent. As these lines are
written, the rate is below 6 percent. Having come so far,
we should face the decade ahead with confidence that we
can travel the short distance that remains.

NOTES

1. After serving the National Wage Stabilization Board as a consul-
tant in 1951, I became the vice-chairman of the board and then the
chairman, 1952–53.

2. The discussion was reviewed in a Study Paper (No. 6) prepared
by the Bureau of Labor Statistics, U.S. Department of Labor, for the
Study of Employment, Growth, and Price Levels by the Joint
Economic Committee of the Congress. The paper was entitled "The
Extent and Nature of Frictional Unemployment" (86th Cong., 1st
Sess., Nov. 19, 1959).

3. The CEA position was most fully developed in Hearings before
the Subcommittee on Employment and Manpower of the Committee
on Labor and Public Welfare, U.S. Senate, 88th Cong., 1st Sess., Part
5, pp. 1769–96. A somewhat revised version of the same presentation

appears in *Economic Report* for 1963 (published January 1964), as Appendix A, pp. 166–90.

4. *Higher Unemployment Rates, 1957–60: Structural Transformation or Inadequate Demand,* Subcommittee on Economic Statistics, Joint Economic Committee, U.S. Congress, 87th Cong., 1st Sess. (Washington, D.C.: U.S. Government Printing Office, 1961).

5. See note 3 above.

6. Friendly critics have advised me that this kind of criticism is in very poor taste. Perhaps so. But I think even stronger criticism could easily be justified. Not only the authors of the articles in question were misled but so also were the editors and referees of the leading journals in the field.

7. In my first major presentation on structural unemployment I described a model quite different from that of the JEC study paper. Hearings before the Subcommittee on Employment and Manpower of the Committee on Labor and Public Welfare, U.S. Senate, 88th Cong., 1st Sess., Part 5, pp. 1461–1511. There was detailed criticism of the JEC-CEA "structural hypothesis" in my article "Structural Unemployment in the United States," in *Employment Problems of Automation and Advanced Technology,* ed. J. Stieber (New York: St. Martin's Press, 1966), pp. 148–51. See also, as examples, Eleanor G. Gilpatrick, *Structural Unemployment and Aggregate Demand* (Baltimore: Johns Hopkins Press, 1966), pp. 10–14; and R. G. Lipsey, "Structural and Deficiency-Demand Unemployment Reconsidered," in *Employment Policy and the World Market,* ed. A. M. Ross (Berkeley: University of California Press, 1965), pp. 219–36.

8. A considerable number of illustrative quotations are set forth in the article by myself in collaboration with C. T. King, "Tax Cuts and Employment Policy," in *Job Creation: What Works?* ed. R. Taggert (Salt Lake City: Olympus Publishing Company, 1977), pp. 3–5.

9. *Ibid.,* pp. 1–33; see also my address to the annual meeting of the Industrial Relations Research Association: "The Fall and Rise of the Idea of Structural Unemployment," *Proceedings of the Thirty-First Annual Meeting of the IRRA,* 1978, pp. 1–13.

10. Detailed calculations are set forth in an article by myself and M. R. Killingsworth: "Direct Effects of Unemployment and Training Programs on Employment and Unemployment Statistics," in *Conference Report on Youth Unemployment: Its Measurement and Meaning* (Washington, D.C.: U.S. Government Printing Office, 1978), pp. 249–85.

11. Robert L. Stein, "New Definitions for Employment and Unemployment," *Employment and Earnings and Monthly Report on the Labor Force* (February 1967), pp. 3–27.

12. C. T. King, *The Unemployment Impact of the Vietnam War* (Lexington, Mass.: Heath-Lexington Books, forthcoming).

13. Lester C. Thurow, "Redistribution Aspects of Manpower

Training Programs," in *Manpower Programs in the Policy Mix*, ed. Lloyd Ulman (Baltimore: Johns Hopkins Press, 1973), p. 84.

14. Data from C. T. King, *Unemployment Impact*, note 12 above.

15. Unlike the industrial and occupational classifications, educational attainment is a characteristic which does not change significantly among adults. It is a fixed characteristic. It is also related to certain other determinants of socioeconomic status: those with little education usually have had parents with even less education and with low incomes, while the opposite is generally true of college graduates.

16. My 1963 presentation to the Senate Subcommittee (see note 7 above) included a technical note explaining the derivation of the 1950 figures. Figures for later years are derived from regular reports issued by the Bureau of Labor Statistics, U.S. Department of Labor, based on the Current Population Surveys of the Census Bureau. Educational attainment is surveyed annually in March; the figures for 1962, for example, are actually for March 1962, and the same is true for other years. The BLS reports on educational attainment are published first in the *Monthly Labor Review* and then later, with supplementary tables, in the Special Labor Force Reports series.

17. Derived from reports of the U.S. Department of Commerce.

18. Data provided by Placement Office, Michigan State University. MSU does have one of the largest colleges of education in the country, but total enrollment at MSU is also among the largest in the U.S.

19. The best brief survey of the evaluation studies is a policy statement issued by the National Council on Employment Policy, "The Impact of Employment and Training Programs," November 1976. The author of this statement, although his name is not listed as such on the title page, is Robert Taggart.

20. Herman P. Miller, "Critique of David Farber's Method of Evaluating the Gains in Earnings of MDTA Trainees," mimeographed (National Council on Employment Policy, September 1972).

21. George Johnson and James Tomola, "The Fiscal Substitution Effect of Alternative Approaches to Public Service Employment Policy," *The Journal of Human Resources* 12 (winter 1977): 3–26.

22. Michael Borus and Daniel Hamermesh, "Study of the Net Employment Effects of Public Service Employment—Econometric Analyses," in *An Interim Report to the Congress of the National Commission for Manpower Policy, Job Creation through Public Service Employment*, vol. 3, Commissioned Papers (Washington, D.C.: U.S. Government Printing Office, 1978), p. 130.

23. Richard P. Nathan and others, "Monitoring the Public Service Employment Program: The Second Round." Second Report on the Brookings Institution Monitoring Study of the Public Service Employment Program for the National Commission for Employment Policy, March 1979, p. 49.

24. This statement is based on personal interviews with Congressional Budget Office staff members.

25. Congressional Budget Office, *Temporary Measures to Stimulate Employment: An Evaluation of Some Alternatives* (Washington, D.C.: U.S. Government Printing Office, 1975).

26. The CBO presents its estimates in the form of a range of values, and the estimates refer to effects after 24 months. I have used the approximate midpoint of the range estimates.

27. The illustration is oversimplified, simply to economize space. For a more complete treatment, including a discussion of the effect of assuming a 40 percent fiscal substitution rate in the PSE program, see Killingsworth and King, "Tax Cuts and Employment Policy" (note 8 above), pp. 26–28. Such substitution would reduce the direct job-creation effect of PSE to 600,000 jobs, but the direct job creation in the private sector would still be the same: 320,000. Hence, under this assumption total job creation by PSE would be 920,000, and the jobs created in the private sector by PSE would still equal those created by the tax cut.

28. In the light of the Brookings study (see note 23 above) a 40 percent substitution rate appears to be much too high. A rate of 15 to 20 percent would be consistent with the Brookings findings.

29. Harvey Brenner, "Estimating the Social Costs of National Economic Policy: Implications for Mental and Physical Health, and Criminal Aggression," Paper No. 5, *Achieving the Goals of the Employment Act of 1946 —Thirtieth Anniversary Review.* Joint Economic Committee, 94th Cong., 2d sess. (Washington, D.C.: U.S. Government Printing Office, 1976).

Stagflation, Productivity, and the Labor Market

Lester C. Thurow

I. Needed: An Explanation for Inflation and Unemployment

STANDARD NEOCLASSICAL LABOR economics is based upon four basic assumptions about the characteristics of the labor market. (1) Skills are exogenously acquired and then sold in a competitive market. (2) The productivity of each individual worker is known and fixed. (3) Each individual worker has an independent utility function which depends upon his or her own income. And (4) total output is simply the summation of individual productivities.

If these four postulates were true, the U.S. economy could not suffer from an extended period of either unemployment or inflation. If some shock were to cause unemployment, it would disappear as wages fell in response to workers competing for jobs. With lower wages some workers would leave the labor market (leisure would now be more valuable than work), and others would be reabsorbed into employment at the new lower wages. Inflation would disappear for a similar reason. If some price were to go up (say oil due to OPEC), a larger fraction of income would have to be allocated to purchasing oil and a smaller fraction would be left for other goods and services. Since individuals would be buying less, excess capacity would emerge, and the prices of these other goods would fall as companies competed for customers. The higher price of oil would be countered by lower prices in the rest of the economy, and inflation would disappear. Since inflation and unemployment do not disappear in the prescribed manner, it is necessary to go back and reexamine the basic postulates upon which this analysis is built. Upon reexamination, each of the four postulates is seen to be wrong.

(1) Instead of being exogenously acquired, much of our human capital is acquired endogenously on the job. This can be seen in the analysis of earnings functions where on-the-job training variables are seen as increasingly important or in the surveys of the President's Commission on Automation.[1] Sixty percent of the. work force reported that they are using no skills exogenously acquired in formal education or training, and only 12 percent listed formal education and training as the best way to learn the job skills that they were employing.

(2) Instead of being fixed and known, individual productivity is variable and difficult to know. Each worker has a maximum productivity, but depending on motivation they can provide any productivity between that maximum and zero. Employers find it difficult and expensive to know how much productivity each of their employees is providing. And even if they do know, it is difficult and expensive to change wage rates or fire an employee. As a result, every industrial operation requires a substantial component of voluntary cooperation. If employees choose to withhold that voluntary cooperation (work to rule), any industrial operation in the country can be brought to its knees. Evidence for the potential variability in productivity can be seen in the

discipline of industrial psychology, business interests in motivation, and introspection.

(3) Instead of having independent preferences, most workers have interdependent preference functions where their satisfaction or utility depends on their income relative to that of their neighbor. Evidence for this can be seen in the sociology literature on relative deprivation and economic surveys as to what causes economic satisfaction.[2] These surveys universally find that people are satisfied or dissatisfied with their economic circumstances depending on their relative income and not on their absolute income.

(4) All industrial operations are subject to a substantial component of team as well as individual productivity. Evidence for this can be seen in the sharp learning curves of new industrial plants. As workers learn to work with each other, costs of production fall dramatically.[3] They develop teamwork and team productivity that is over and above their individual skills and individual productivity. A much more visible version of the same phenomenon can be seen on the sports pages of the nation's press. Players find that they are paid less than someone else, become unhappy, disrupt the team, and cause it to lose more games than it otherwise would. Although it is less visible, the same thing happens in every industrial operation.

But if we replace the four initial labor-market postulates with the four replacement postulates that I have suggested, where does economic analysis lead? Basically, my postulates provide an explanation of two factors that are widely observed in the labor market. (1) Money wages exhibit downward rigidity. They do not fall when surplus labor exists. (2) Relative wages are rigid and change only in the long run. Keynes wrestled with the consequences of rigid money and relative wages, but he never provided an explanation. The four replacement postulates provide an explanation.

Because skills are acquired endogenously on the job in an informal process of one worker training another, every industrial operation needs workers willing to be trainers. But in a competitive world no one wants to be an informal trainer. Every worker realizes that every additional worker trained will result in lower wages and a greater probability of being fired in any economic downturn. It is rational in a competitive world for each individual to seek a monopoly on local knowledge (how to run machine X) and then refuse to share his or her knowledge with anyone else. This preserves wage and job opportunities. To promote training and make workers willing to be trainers of other workers employers essentially offer two guarantees. First, they promise not to lower wages if surplus workers become available. Second, they promise to hire and fire based on seniority. This means that each trainer's trainees will be fired before he is. The employer essentially agrees not to be a short-run cost minimizer in the interests of long-run training and efficiency. But this leads to money wages rigid in a downward direction.

Rigid relative wages spring from interdependent preferences, but these preferences are enforced on the employer through the employee's ability to vary his own productivity and to disrupt team productivity. Because of interdependent preferences workers perceive some wage differentials as fair and other wage differentials as unfair. But they need some threat to force employers to give fair relative wages. In the neoclassical world there would be no way to enforce the interdependent preferences even if they existed. But in the real world employees can cut their own productivity or disrupt team productivity if wage differentials are perceived as unfair.

Employers find it difficult and expensive to determine who is providing less productivity. Firing is expensive and disrupts the team. Even knowing who is at fault does not lead to an easy solution. As a result, employers find it more profitable to pay the wage differentials that employees view as fair than to shift to the wage differentials called for by changes in short-run supplies and demands in the labor market. Total productivity paying "fair" differentials is higher than total productivity paying supply-and-demand differentials since workers can alter the level of productivity depending on their satisfaction or dissatisfaction with pay scales. The net result is a structure of rigid relative wages.

But with downward rigidity in money wages and fixed relative wages, labor markets cannot clear via wage reductions and shifts in relative wages. They clear based upon worker qualifications (level of education and such), but this leaves the economy with unemployment. Workers who are willing to work at current wages cannot find work. Since wages do not fall, prices do not fall, and this lack of price flexibility is compounded by monopoly and oligopoly power on the part of firms. Instead of reducing prices in times of excess capacity, they cut production. This produces more unemployment, but it also causes inflation. When oil prices rise, other prices do not fall. Prices become downwardly rigid, and any exogenous upward shock leads to inflation.

II. A Series of Bad Judgments and Bad Luck

In the late 1960s and early 1970s the U.S. economy experienced a series of such upward shocks. Some of them were caused by our mistakes and bad judgments, and some of them were simply random bad luck. This is not the place to dissect these causes in detail, but let me briefly enumerate some of the main causes.

Our stagflation problems started with President Johnson's misfinancing of the Vietnam War in 1965 and 1966. Taxes were not raised when they should have been raised, and this led to aggregated-demand inflation. But it is important to note that inflationary pressures only gradually accelerated. When President Johnson left office at the end of 1968, inflation was only running at 4.5 percent per year.

The second set of mistakes and bad luck occurred in the 1971–73 period under President Nixon. In an effort to be reelected, President Nixon imposed wage-and-price controls in the late summer of 1971 and then overstimulated the economy with both monetary and fiscal policies from then until November 1972. This allowed him to run for reelection in a period of rapid growth, falling unemployment, and low inflation, but the cost would be added inflation in 1973 and 1974. Compounding this were the Russian crop failure and the decision to sell more grain to the Russians than the U.S. could spare without sharp upward movements in agricultural prices. This effect was in turn further magnified with the corn blight in the U.S. and the decision to leave acreage controls in place for the 1973 crop.

Finally, the problem was further worsened by the decision of OPEC to raise the price of oil in the winter of 1973–74 along with rapidly rising prices for raw materials. The latter were partly caused by simultaneous periods of rapid growth in most of the industrialized world and a combination of panic and speculative buying. The net result of all these factors was double digit inflation in 1973 and 1974.

If you ask what could have been done about inflation in 1974, the answer is probably very little. None of the mistakes or pieces of bad luck could be reversed in 1974. If you make mistakes and have bad luck, you simply have to suffer the consequences. But in the panic of double-digit inflation and the disruption of Watergate, the government adopted the standard remedy for simple aggregate-demand inflation. It used very tight money policies and a credit crunch along with tight fiscal policies to cause the sharpest recession since the Great Depression. Output fell and unemployment approached 9 percent. Thus the unemployment part of stagflation arose in the effort to control inflation.

Unemployment was not going to correct the mistakes of Presidents Johnson or Nixon, and it was not going to offset bad weather, corn blights, or OPEC oil-price increases, but if severe enough it could affect other prices. Partly because of this effect and partly because the upward price shocks were retreating into the past, inflation did in fact fall to 5.5 percent by mid-1975. Although unemployment was above 8 percent and almost 30 percent of our capital capacity was idle, inflation did not continue to fall in 1975 or in later years. It stuck at 5.5 percent through 1975, 1976, and 1977 and then started to rise, even though substantial amounts of idle labor and capital remained. Why?

III. A Shift in the Structure of the Economy

If one seriously asks why idle resources are not reducing the rate of inflation, the answer is not hard to find. It lies in the phenomenon of "indexing" and not in excess aggregate demand. Since 1974 and the scare of double-digit inflation, labor, business, and government have sought to protect themselves from the uncertainties of future inflation by adding cost-of-living indexes to all of their future commitments. Cost-of-living escalators are increasingly being built into government wages and programs. Very few business contracts are currently signed without the protection of inflation escalators. Cost-of-living clauses have become almost universal in new labor-union contracts since 1974. Nonunion workers do not have legal cost-of-living clauses, but companies who provide cost-of-living protection to their unionized workers almost always give the same protection to their nonunion employees. Similarly, nonunion employers de facto index wages to keep their best employees from moving to employers who do index and to keep unions out. Adding cost-of-living escalators to private contracts is a perfectly rational response to inflation on the part of both business and labor, but it fundamentally alters the nature of the economy and the effectiveness of monetary and fiscal policies.

The classic objection to "legal" indexing is that it reduces the effectiveness of monetary and fiscal policies. The reasons are easy to understand. If inflation is 6 percent this year, all wages and prices will go up 6 percent next year due to escalator clauses, but this leads to a 6 percent rate of inflation next year and hence to 6 percent increases in wages and prices in the third year. While only parts of the economy (some government programs and wages) have legally been indexed, there is no difference between government indexing and private indexing when it comes to their impact on macroeconomic policies. The policies still produce unemployment, but they lose their capacity to reduce inflation. They can only reduce the rate of inflation if they are tight enough to produce a basic wage settlement (excluding the cost-of-living clauses) less than the rate of growth of productivity (about 2 percent). Given basic settlements currently far in excess of that level, unemployment would have to be much higher to generate the appropriate settlements.

The impotence of monetary and fiscal policies in a world of private indexing is easiest to demonstrate in the case of monetary policies. Consider the standard quantity theory of money. $MV \equiv PT$ where M is the supply of money, V equals the velocity of money, P equals the price level, and T equals the real GNP. Traditionally we envision the direction of causation flowing from MV to PT. An increase in MV leads to an increase in P and/or T. In a Phillips curve world any increase in MV leads to greater increases in P and smaller increases in T as the rate of unemployment drops. In a natural rate of unemployment world the rate of increases of P falls if unemployment is above the natural rate, and the rate of increases of P rises if unemployment is below the natural rate. At the natural rate of unemployment P rises at some constant rate which may be high or low. But it does not accelerate or decelerate. Monetary policies help to determine in which of these areas the economy operates.

But what happens in a world which is completely indexed? Now the direction of causation is reversed. P is rising at some rate, say 6 percent, due to indexing. Given a P rising at 6 percent, the monetary authorities have two choices. First, they can adjust the money supply to hold MV constant. By doing so, however, they will not reduce the rate of increase of P. They will only reduce the real GNP, T, and produce higher unemployment. Their second choice is to accommodate the 6 percent price increase and allow MV to rise by 6 percent. This does not produce unemployment but also does not produce a lower rate of inflation. As long as the indexing is in place, monetary authorities cannot reduce the rate of inflation. They control the rate of unemployment but not the rate of inflation.

But there is an added problem. Any upward price shocks will be built into the index and carried forward into the future. If further oil-price increases lead the rate of inflation to rise from 5.5 percent to 6 percent, then indexing will carry the 6 percent inflation forward into the future since wages and prices will now rise by 6 percent per year rather than 5.5 percent per year. As the data in table 1 show, such upward shocks occurred in 1978 and raised the rate of inflation into the 8 percent range. About half of these shocks were also caused by government policies. Food prices were raised by agricultural price supports, home ownership costs were principally affected by higher interest rates, and both the

Table 1

What Made Inflation Worse?
(Consumer prices, percent change)

		1978
The Trend Inflation Rate		5.3
—was aggravated by:		
Food Prices		0.7
– Policy	0.3	
– Livestock	0.4	
The Dollar		0.4
Minimum Wage		0.1
Social Security and Other Policy		0.3
Homeownership		0.6
Demand		0.3
Actual change in consumer prices		7.7

Source: *Data Resources Review*, January 1979.

minimum wage increase and the Social Security tax increases were direct government policies.

Since additional minimum-wage and social-security-tax increases are scheduled for 1979, another round of upward price shocks will occur. These will also be built into the base rate of inflation and lead to even higher rates of inflation in 1980. And as it happens, conventional monetary and fiscal policies will be powerless to prevent it. But before going on to analyse the steps that might be taken to lower the rate of inflation, let us stop to look at the impacts of inflation.

IV. Stagflation and the Distribution of Real Economic Resources

Inflation is the paradigm zero-sum game. Whenever a price goes up, two things happen. Whoever buys that particular commodity finds that his or her real income goes down. But someone also gets that extra income. It may be the seller, the producer (capital or labor), or the owner of raw materials, but no income is thrown away. As a result, for every loser there must be a winner. Inflation can redistribute income, but it cannot lower aggregate real income.

In addition to telling us who has won and who has lost, an analysis of the distribution of income can tell us something about the characteristics of the economy. Do government programs work to cushion income shocks from unemployment and inflation? Who enjoys the protection of de facto and de jure indexing and who does not?

A. The Distribution of Real Income Flows

Since inflation in its virulent form broke out in 1973,

1972 will be taken as the base year for the purposes of analysing the effects of stagflation. Wage-and-price controls were in effect in 1972, but 1972 seems to be a normal year in that the distribution of economic resources was very close to what it had been over the previous decade. 1972 also has the advantage that it is a year in which we have measures of the distribution of wealth.

As the data in table 2 indicate, the inflation rate accelerated from 4.1 percent in 1972 to 9.7 percent in 1974, fell to 5.2 percent in 1976, and then reaccelerated to an annual rate of 8.4 percent in the first three quarters of 1978. With the very strong monetary and fiscal stimulus of 1972, unemployment was falling in 1972 from 5.6 percent to 4.9 percent in 1973. In the recession of 1974-75 it rose to 8.5 percent and since then has been gradually falling to the 6.0 percent level reached in the third quarter of 1978.

From 1972 to 1978 real disposable personal income

Table 2

Year	Implicit Price Deflator for GNP	Unemployment Rate
1972	4.1%	5.6%
1973	5.9	4.9
1974	9.7	5.6
1975	9.6	8.5
1976	5.2	7.7
1977	5.9	7.0
1978	7.4	6.0

Source: *Survey of Current Business and Employment and Earnings* (1979).

per capita has risen 15 percent. After accounting for inflation, taxes, and population growth, real incomes have gone up, not down. Real incomes fell at the height of the recession in 1974 and 1975 but have since recovered sharply. Somewhat surprisingly, if you compare the real income gain in the six years since 1972 with the real income gain in the six years prior to 1972, you find that real incomes went up by only 17 percent in the earlier period. Real standards of living were rising somewhat faster prior to 1972 than after 1972, but the difference is not large.

Where the real difference comes, however, is in the gains in money incomes. In the first period disposable per-capita personal incomes rose 51.0 percent, and in the second period they rose 73 percent—2.8 times as rapidly as real incomes in the first period and 4.8 times as rapidly as in the second period. While money illusion is not supposed to bother anyone in a world populated with the rational "homo economicus," it is difficult to avoid coming to the conclusion that part of the dissatisfaction with the performance of the economy in the last six years is due to money illusion. People get dissatisfied if someone deposits $73 on their doorstep and then takes $58 away from them in the form of higher prices. They may even be able to convince themselves that their real standards of living have gone down. And in some psychological sense they may be worse off. The real income gains may not be much different than they had been in the past, but everyone thinks how enjoyable their life would be if there were no inflation and money income continued to go up at the same rate.

While a world with a 73 percent rise in real incomes every six years would be much less frustrating than the world that actually exists, it is also an unattainable, imaginary world. Most Americans tend to forget that inflation raises incomes as well as prices. Every price increase is a reduction in the real living standard of some purchaser of a good or service, but it is also a real income increase for some provider of that good or service. The money it takes to pay higher prices does not disappear. It goes to someone. Since inflation is a zero-sum game, the only question is to identify the winners and losers. And since there are a number of ways that the economy could be subdivided, there also are a number of ways that the winners and losers can be classified.

B. The Functional Distribution of Income

First, look at the functional distribution of income among corporate business, persons, and governments. Table 3 shows the gross and net distribution of the GNP. The difference between the gross and net figures reflects the transfers between the sectors. Dividends and interest are deducted from the gross cash flows going to corporations to yield a net cash flow. Transfer payments, interest payments, and business subsidies are deducted from the gross government share to get a net government share. In addition, grants-in-aid are subtracted from the gross federal government share and added to the net state and local share to yield a net share for each level of government. The aim is to find a net income share that essentially corresponds to disposable personal income as modified by the income flow going to noncorporate business. The net income is that income which the sector can spend after it has made all of the transfers that it "needs" to make.

In the period since 1972 the gross share going to corporations has remained essentially unchanged (10.0 versus 9.8). If the recession-induced 8.3 percent share in 1974 is excluded, the gross corporate share averaged 10.1 percent from 1973 through 1978.

Table 3

GNP Shares

Year	Corporate Business		Persons		Government		Federal		State and Local	
	Gross	Net	Gross	Net	Gross	Net	Gross	Net	Gross	Net
1972	10.0%	7.6%	58.6%	71.1%	31.4%	21.3%	19.4%	7.2%	12.0%	14.1%
1973	9.7	7.1	58.8	71.8	31.5	21.1	19.7	7.3	11.8	13.8
1974	8.3	5.7	59.5	73.1	32.2	21.2	20.4	7.1	11.8	14.1
1975	10.2	7.3	59.2	74.5	30.6	17.9	18.7	3.4	11.9	14.5
1976	10.4	7.8	58.0	73.0	31.6	19.2	19.5	4.5	12.1	14.7
1977	10.3	7.7	57.7	72.4	32.0	19.9	19.8	5.1	12.2	14.8
1978*	9.8	7.1	58.0	72.7	32.2	20.2	20.1	5.4	12.1	14.8
Average										
1973–78	9.8	7.1	58.6	73.0	31.6	19.9	19.7	5.5	11.9	14.4

*Average of first and second quarters.

Source: *Survey of Current Business* (1979).

Although there has not been a statistically significant shift in the gross corporate share, there has been a decline in the net corporate share from 7.6 percent to 7.1 percent. This decline is even more noticeable if one looks back at the period of time when the gross corporate share was 10.6 percent and the net corporate share was 8.2 percent. Thus there has been some long-run slippage in the gross corporate share, but it occurred well before the outbreak of rapid inflation in 1973. The slippage in the net share, however, has been twice as large as the slippage in the gross share. This can be traced to the rise in interest payments. In the 1964–68 period corporate business was making net interest payments equal to 0.6 percent of the GNP. Thus higher interest rates are the primary cause of a lower net corporate share. Since these higher interest rates were caused by the efforts to fight inflation, inflation can be said to have lowered the net corporate share but not the gross corporate share.

If you look at gross government shares, there are also no discernible trends for either federal or state and local governments. With the rise of transfer payments, grants-in-aid, business subsidies, and interest payments there has, however, been a noticeable shift in the net federal government share. It has declined from 7.2 percent in 1972 to an average of 5.5 percent in the period after 1972 and 5.4 percent in 1978.

If the net corporate share is falling and the net federal government share is falling, then either the net state and local share or the net personal share must be rising. As the data show, there has been a small increase in the net state and local government share, but most of the increase has occurred in the share of personal income. The net personal income share has risen 1.6 percent, from 71.1 percent to 72.7 percent. On balance, persons have gained vis-à-vis both corporations and governments in the period of stagflation since 1972.

C. Rich Versus Poor

Table 4 shows the distribution of money income from families and unrelated individuals for 1972 and 1977. The data in between are not shown since they are essentially identical with those at the end points. Given the sampling errors that occur, these data show essentially no change in the distribution of money incomes between rich and poor. The top 40 percent of the population had 69.5 percent of total income in 1972 and 69.6 percent in 1977. The bottom 40 percent of the population had 13.7 percent in 1972 and 13.8 percent in 1977. While the changes are not large enough to be statistically significant, there may have been a very small shift in income toward the bottom 20 percent and the fourth quintile (60th to 80th percentiles).

While the distribution of money income has not been altered by stagflation, the charge is often made that the distribution of real income has been altered since the cost of living has gone up faster for low-income groups which spend more of their income on those goods and services (food, fuel, and such) that have gone up the most in price. When cost-of-living indexes are calculated for

Table 4

Distribution of Money Income

Quintile	1972	1977
First	3.7%	4.0%
Second	10.0	9.8
Third	16.9	16.6
Fourth	24.7	25.1
Fifth	44.8	44.5

each of the five quintiles, this charge is not substantiated. From 1972 to 1977 the implicit price deflator for personal consumption expenditures rose by 39.0 percent (see table 5). No quintile, however, has experienced a rise in their cost of living that is more than 0.5 percentage points away from this average. Converting the money distribution of income to a real distribution of income does not change the conclusion that there has been essentially no change in the distribution of income among rich and poor.

Another argument that is often heard revolves around the progressivity of the federal income tax. In a period of inflation individual taxpayers move up the progressive rate structure since taxes are levied on money income. This leads to a higher level of taxes on real income. While the argument is certainly correct if everything else remains the same, everything else does not remain the same. More individuals itemize their deductions (which also rise with inflation), and Congress periodically cuts taxes to offset the impact of inflation.

Table 5[4]

Personal Consumption Implicit-Price Deflators for Personal Consumption, 1972–77
(1972 = 100.0)

Quintile	
First	139.0
Second	139.5
Third	138.9
Fourth	138.6
Fifth	138.9
Total:	139.0

When one actually analyses the data, the latter effects more than offset the former effects. Federal personal-income taxes have fallen from 10.9 percent of personal income in 1972 to 10.6 percent of personal income in the first half of 1978 (see table 6). Average tax collections from 1973 through 1978 amounted to 10.4 percent. Thus the aggregate federal income-tax burden is down, not up.

While the aggregate burden is not up, it would be possible to increase the burden on some income classes. Here again, if we look at the actual data there is no evidence of a shift in tax burdens among the income classes. The share of total federal income taxes paid by the bottom 40 percent of the population fell from 9.8 percent to 9.6 percent from 1972 to 1975 (the last year for which IRS data is available), while the share of total taxes paid by the top 40 percent rose from 77.7 to 77.9 percent (see table 6). The changes are both small and well within the realm of random error in measurements.

D. Age, Sex, and Racial Groups

According to the data generated by the *Current Population Reports,* the distribution of income has been subject to only very small changes if one looks at the distribution of income among the normal socioeconomic groups. From 1972 to 1977 the percentage of the population living below the official poverty line has declined from 11.9 percent to 11.6 percent. Black household incomes have risen from 58 to 59 percent of whites. Data on Hispanic households is not available for 1972, but their relative income has risen from 71 percent to 75 percent of that of whites from 1973 to 1977. Low-income groups have not gained in the 1970s as they did in the 1960s, but they also have not been falling behind. High unemployment and slower real growth have stopped them from catching up with the mainstream of the economy, but these groups have not been forced back to the levels of relative income that existed in the early 1960s.

Farm-household incomes rose from 81 to 87 percent of nonfarm incomes from 1972 to 1977. Relative incomes were higher during the years of peak agricultural prices, but farmers are better off now than they were at the beginning of the period.

Since elderly incomes are much more skewed than the incomes of the rest of the population, the relative position of elderly households depends upon whether you look at mean or median household incomes. Per-capita

Table 6

The Burden of Federal Income Taxes

Percent of Personal Income		Distribution of Federal Income Tax Burdens		
Year		Quintile	1972	1975
1972	10.9%	First	2.6%	2.6%
1973	10.4	Second	7.2	7.0
1974	10.9	Third	12.5	12.5
1975	9.6	Fourth	19.9	19.5
1976	10.2	Fifth	57.8	58.4
1977	10.6			
1978*	10.6			
Average				
1973–78	10.4			

*First six months.

Source: *Survey of Current Business* and IRS *Statistics of Income, Individual Income Tax Returns* (1978).

mean household incomes for the elderly fell insignificantly from 94 percent to 93 percent of that of the entire population from 1972 to 1977. Per-capita median household incomes rose slightly from 72 percent to 75 percent of that of the entire population over the same time period. Social security payments are also heavily underreported in the income data in the *Current Population Reports.* If one corrects for this underreporting, in 1972 and 1977 per-capita mean elderly household incomes hold constant at 100 percent of that of the rest of the entire population. Per-capita median household incomes rose from 80 to 85 percent of that of the entire population. As a result, it seems clear that the elderly have in fact improved their relative income position during the course of the period with high inflation.

If you look at the earnings of full-time, year-round female workers relative to the equivalent male group, there has been essentially no change, with females earning 58 percent of what men earned in 1972 and 57 percent in 1977.

Since almost half of those unemployed in the United States are 16 to 24 years of age and since many of these new entrants into the labor market are not eligible for unemployment insurance, one would expect that stagflation would have had a serious effect on their relative income. But when one looks at the data, the effects are not what one would expect. Since participation rates are rising for the 16–24-year-old age group, the percentages of the population in this age group with no income fell from 1972 to 1977. For males the percentage fell from 6 to 5 percent. For females the percentage with no income fell from 51 to 45 percent for the younger age group and from 22 to 16 percent for the older age group.

Among males with income relative incomes were constant at 11 percent for the 14–19 age group and 62 percent for the 20–24 age group in both 1972 and 1977. If one looks at full-time, year-round workers, the 14–19-year-old age group earned 40 percent as much as all males who work full-time year-round in both 1972 and 1977, and the relative income of the 20–24-year-old age group slipped only slightly from 67 percent in 1972 to 65 percent in 1977. For 14–19-year-old females, relative incomes rose from 21 to 24 percent of all females, and for those who worked full-time year-round, relative earnings rose from 62 to 64 percent. Among the 20–24-year-old females there is some slippage in relative earnings: relative income fell from 111 to 104 percent of total female income; among those who work full-time year-round, relative income fell from 89 to 85 percent. Thus the only significant change is a deterioration in the relative incomes of 20–24-year-old females.

The overall conclusion is clear. In the period since 1972 there has been either a slight improvement or consistency in the relative position of low-income groups. Otherwise, relative positions have remained approximately constant. Stagflation has not altered the distribution of income in any significant way.

E. The Distribution of Net Worth

What has stagflation done to the distribution of net worth in physical assets? Since the generation of official net-worth statistics is a process with long lags (the most recent official data are for 1972), it is not as easy to check on the changes in the distribution of net worth as it is on the changes in the distribution of income. It is, however, possible to make some calculations that shed light on what has probably happened to the distribution of net worth.

While we do not have direct data on the distribution of

net worth in 1977, we do have data on the holdings of different types of assets (stocks, bonds, real estate, and such) by wealth classes in 1972 and what has happened to the aggregate value of these different types of assets between 1972 and 1977. If you assume that the average investment ability is equal in each net-worth class or that financial markets are a random walk, then we would expect the value for each type of asset in each net-worth class to advance or fall by the same amount as the aggregate gains or losses for this type of asset for the country as a whole.[5]

Since the last wealth survey of the entire population is now 16 years out-of-date, I will limit myself to analysing what the Internal Revenue Service calls top wealthholders. Top wealthholders are that group which will have to file federal estate-tax returns when they die. Top wealthholders amount to 6.1 percent of the population, but they own approximately 65 percent of all of the privately held net worth in the United States. Thus a quintile of the top wealthholders amounts to approximately 1.2 percent of the total population. As the data in table 7 indicate, there is a very skewed distribution of wealth even among these top wealthholders. The first quintile owns 1.9 percent of the total wealth held by the group, and the top quintile owns 62.5 percent of the total wealth. If we extrapolate the holdings of each wealth class forward to 1977 based on their 1972 portfolios and the 1972 to 1977 increases or decreases in aggregate values for each type of asset, there has been a noticeable change in the distribution of net worth. The top quintile has lost 1.9 percent of total net worth, and the bottom quintile has lost 0.4 percent of total net worth. The second quintile has gained 0.6 percentage points, the third quintile has gained 0.8 percentage points, and the fourth quintile has gained 0.9 percentage points.

If you ask the reasons for these changes, there is a very simple explanation. Most of the different types of assets have gone up in value and by approximately the same amount, but there is a huge exception: corporate stocks. The value of corporate stocks has gone down by 10.9 percent during the 1972–77 period. The richer you are, the larger corporate stock looms as a fraction of your portfolio; and thus the richer you are, the greater are your losses on corporate stock. The distribution of net worth has changed, not because the middle quintiles have made gains in their ownership of assets, but because the very top of the wealth distribution has suffered losses.

The bottom quintile has suffered losses in its share of total assets since it includes those who have enough gross assets to be included in a list of the top wealthholders but who have a negative net worth. With stagflation the number and size of negative net-worth individuals has increased.

If you look at the changes in mean real net worth by

Table 7

Distribution of Net Worth for Top Wealthholders

Quintile	1972		1977	
First	1.9%		1.5%	
Second	8.3		8.9	
Third	11.0	35.6	11.8	37.9
Fourth	16.3		17.2	
Fifth	62.5		60.6	

Source: Internal Revenue Service, *Personal Wealth, 1972* (Washington, D.C.: Government Printing Office, 1972).

income class, you can see that top wealthholders as a group lost 5 percent of their assets (see table 8). Most of this occurred because of losses on corporate stock, but note noncorporate equity has advanced at a rate less than the rate of inflation. Basically, the middle of the net-worth distribution has broken even with rising losses as you move out into either the lower or upper tails. The negative net worth of those with negative net worth rose 25 percent, and the net worth of those with over $5 million in net worth in 1972 declined 14 percent.

While the performance of the stock market has led to a decline in real net worth, it is harder to blame this result on the onset of stagflation in 1973. By using the implicit price deflator for personal-consumption expenditures, you see that stock prices peaked in 1968 and have declined 29 percent since then. Declining real stock values continued during the stagflation, but it actually slowed relative to the pace of the previous four years.

F. The Bottom Line

If you look at the functional and personal distribution of the GNP, it is clear that the period of stagflation that we have had since 1972 has made surprisingly little difference. This tells us two things about the economy. First, the impacts of high unemployment have been extensively cushioned by government transfer payments. Second, inflation seems to have had little if any impact on the distribution of income. This means that the economy is heavily de jure or de facto indexed. If indexing had not occurred, we would have seen major changes in the distribution of income.

Indexing is a peculiar phenomenon, however, in that it both undercuts the seriousness of inflation and makes it harder to stop inflation. In an indexed world both

Table 8

Changes in Average Real and Nominal Net Worth

1972 Net Worth (Class $'000)	Percent of Population	Mean Nominal Net Worth ($'000) 1972	1977	Real Net Worth (1972 dollars) 1977	% Change
negative	0.05	-216	-379	-269	-25
0 - 20	.43	12	14	10	-11
20 - 50	.89	37	50	36	-2
50 - 60	.42	55	79	56	-1
60 - 70	.70	65	94	67	-2
70 - 80	.53	74	108	77	-1
80 - 100	.79	89	129	92	0
100 - 150	.99	121	162	115	-5
150 - 250	.65	189	262	186	-2
250 - 500	.40	340	449	319	-6
500 - 1000	.15	681	857	609	-11
1000 - 5000	.08	1,817	2,266	1,610	-11
5000 +	.005	9,805	11,875	8,440	-14
total	6.1	144	193	137	-5%

Source: Internal Revenue Service, *Personal Wealth, 1972* (Washington, D.C.: Government Printing Office, 1972).

monetary and fiscal policies lose much of their antiin-flationary impact. In an indexed world tight monetary and fiscal policies lead to large reductions in the real GNP and only small reductions in the price level.

The largest changes in the distribution of real economic resources has occurred in the distribution of real net worth. Real net worth is down by 5 percent with even larger losses for small and large net-worth holders. The decline in real corporate stock values explains most of this result, but this decline started well before the period of stagflation and has in fact decelerated during the period of stagflation. Since the gross after-tax share of the GNP going to corporate business has not declined, the result must be explained by changes in the evaluation of corporate earnings rather than in declining earnings themselves. Higher interest rates and higher uncertainty premiums can certainly lead to the capitalization of earnings streams at lower multiples, and stagflation can certainly lead to both higher interest rates and higher uncertainty premiums. Interest rates go up in the battle to fight inflation, and the possibility of government-induced recessions raises the uncertainty premium.

If this is the correct explanation for declining real net worth, then future declines should be expected in view of current economic policies. Interest rates have been deliberately raised, and in the process the probability of a recession has been greatly increased. The net result is a higher discount rate and lower net worths even though the functional distribution of income has not shifted.

V. An Uneven Structure of Unemployment

At the beginning of 1979 many analysts were arguing that the economy was at full employment despite a-6 percent overall rate of unemployment. Even the 1979 Economic Report of the President expressed some sympathy with this position. The argument flows from the observation that the structure of unemployment is very uneven. At one extreme minority teen-agers have unemployment rates near 60 percent (when adjustments are made for those minority youth who have dropped out of the economic system) and at the other extreme prime-age (25–55) white males have unemployment rates of 2.5 percent. Almost 50 percent of all those officially unemployed are 16 to 24 years of age. Those who argue that 6 percent unemployment is in fact full employment point to the 2.5 percent and argue that since the economy has run out of prime-age white males, it is at full employment.

One can quibble as to whether a 2.5 percent rate for prime-age white males is really full employment for this group (their unemployment rate reached 1.2 percent in 1969), but there is no denying a very uneven structure of unemployment with women, adult blacks, Hispanics, elderly whites, and young whites ranged between the extremes of black teen-agers and prime-age white males.

This uneven structure of unemployment brings us back to the four basic postulates of labor economics. If the four basic postulates of neoclassical labor markets were correct, such an uneven structure of unemployment could not exist. Labor shortage would cause the relative wages of prime-age white males to rise, and labor surpluses would cause the wages of the rest of the labor force to fall. As a result employers would hire fewer prime-age white males and more of the rest of the labor force. Unemployment would rise for prime-age white males, and unemployment would fall for the rest of the labor force.

In fact, the uneven structure has not been disappearing but growing worse over the decade of the 1970s. This can only be explained in a world in which you think of (1) skills being exogenously acquired on the job, (2) productivity being individually variable, (3) interdependent preferences, and (4) team productivity. These four factors lead to rigid relative wages. With rigid relative wages there are no incentives for employers to shift their patterns of employment. And with skills being acquired exogenously on the job, seniority hiring and firing, and normal labor-force turnover, unemployment becomes more and more concentrated among the young, the elderly, minorities, and women as time passes.

This phenomenon is particularly dramatic if you couple the high youth unemployment rates that have been outlined in this section with the changes in relative wage rates that were outlined in the previous section. Despite an extended period of high unemployment the relative earnings of young people have not declined. The four basic postulates of neoclassical labor economics offer no explanation for the rigidity of relative wages. The alternative four postulates provide an easy answer.

While there is an easy explanation for the uneven structure of unemployment, this does not mean that there is an easy solution. One solution would be to reverse the process that created the current uneven structure of unemployment. Monetary and fiscal policies would be used to stimulate the demand for labor until there was in fact a shortage of prime-age white males. With a shortage of prime-age white males, employers would be forced to hire a larger fraction of their labor force from among other members of the labor force, and in the process the differentials in unemployment rates would narrow. While there is no doubt that such a procedure would work, there is also no doubt that such a procedure would cause even more inflation than now exists.

Conservatives often argue that youth unemployment could easily be solved by eliminating the minimum wage or by establishing a lower minimum wage for young people than for adults. While the minimum wage certainly does not contribute to solving the problem, youth unemployment cannot be traced to the minimum wage nor can it be eliminated by altering the minimum-wage law.

Minimum wages have two effects. They raise earnings for some and produce unemployment for others. Unemployment occurs when an individual's productivity exceeds the previous minimum wage but falls below the new minimum wage. Those whose productivity is below the new minimum wage are fired since they now represent a net loss as far as the employer is concerned. The real question, however, is not the existence of such an effect, but its size.

If one reviews the econometric literature on the quantitative impact of the minimum wage, one is driven to the conclusion that the impact is small and does not explain much of youth unemployment. As a report of the Congressional Budget Office noted, when allowances are made for the growth of the teen-age labor force, no statistically significant correlations have been found between youth employment and the minimum wage.[6] This is not to say that no one is unemployed as a result, but the inability of diligent searchers to find a strong significant effect indicates that the effect is relatively small. If it were large, it would be easy to find.

But there are also less technical ways of seeing the same phenomenon. For many years Western European countries were pointed out as examples of countries where a better articulation between school and work and dual minimum wages (lower for young people) led to lower youth unemployment rates. But in the current recession youth unemployment in many of these countries has risen to, or even above, American rates. Lower youth minimum wages and better youth placement and training have not solved the problem. When there is a shortage of jobs, young people end up with more than their proportional share of unemployment. "Last hired; first fired" rules lead quite naturally to unemployment for younger workers. Without a growing pool of jobs new entrants into the labor market cannot find their first job, and new entrants are predominantly young.

The unimportance of the minimum wage is also visible in the. lack of employer interest in provisions ˙of the minimum wage that *now* allow employers to pay lower wages. Under the current minimum wage laws employers can pay 75 percent of the minimum wage to student learners, apprentices, messengers, and full-time students. Yet in 1975 only 40 percent of the 200,000 places that had been authorized were filled. If lowering the minimum wage were to make a big difference in employer hiring desires, there would be a lot more applications for the right to pay less than the minimum wage and full use of the permissions granted.

The minimum wage laws are also widely violated by small employers. Why should they not be? There are no penalties other than having to come into compliance with the law. No fines are levied, no criminal sentences are handed out, and the government does not even require the payment of back wages due (it gives evidence to individual employees who may then, if they wish and can afford it, go into court to collect back wages due). Given such law, it would be very surprising if it had any major impact on the economy.

In any case, whatever one believes about the impact of the minimum wage, it has not aggravated the problem of youth unemployment in the immediate past. Like all other economic prices, the impact of the minimum wage depends upon its level relative to other prices or, more specifically, other wages. Relative to the average wage, the minimum wage has been lower in the 1970s than it was through most of the 1950s and 1960s. In relative terms the minimum wage has gone down, not up. Therefore, the employment handicap that it imposes on young workers must be less now than it was then. If anything, changes in the minimum wage, or, more accurately, the lack of changes in the minimum wage, have improved the employment position of young workers. The real problem as we have seen is, not the minimum wage, but rigid relative wages. Youth employment suffers from a relative wage which is too high, but this wage is not caused by the minimum wage.

But what can be done? If the structure of unemployment prevents monetary and fiscal policies from being used to reduce unemployment, then the structure of unemployment must be altered. Since there are no practical policies for changing relative labor supplies, the policy options must lie on the demand side of the market. Here there are two choices. Either one can issue a set of commands ordering people to change their hiring practices or one can adopt a system of wage subsidies designed to entice employers to change their hiring practices. Realistically this means there is only one option: the wage subsidy.

Basically the wage subsidy is like a reduction in the minimum wage without the disadvantages that such a reduction entails. Employers respond to a lower net wage in either case, but with a wage subsidy all employers, not just those who hire at the minimum wage, have an incentive to employ relatively more workers from economic minorities. Minority workers also do not face a sharply lower wage rate with the resultant reduction in work incentives and decreases in absolute and relative incomes. It is consistent with progress toward economic integration and income parity.

While there are many legitimate objections to wage subsidies—much of the subsidy will be given for employment that would have taken place without the subsidy, and so on—all other solutions are worse. The objections are also equally applicable to the 10 percent investment tax credit. Yet the latter is a favorite conservative economic policy, while the former is usually treated as some radical departure from sound economic practice. The wage subsidy can also be viewed as an offset necessary to eliminate some of the biases toward capital and away from labor caused by the investment tax credit and payroll taxation to finance social security.

Part of the reason that the minimum wage does not have more of an effect than it does have is that most employers—and practically all large employers—have de facto minimum wages which are far above the legal minimum wage. These private minimum wages may be negotiated in labor-union contracts or be a competitive necessity to get the quality of labor the employer desires. A lower legal minimum wage simply would not make any difference to most employers—and all of the best employers. In contrast, a wage subsidy encourages everyone to hire more young people. A general wage subsidy rather than a lower legal minimum wage also gets around the argument that the program is really being run for the benefit of low-wage nonunion employers who provide little or no training and few lifetime career opportunities.

With a wage subsidy program it is possible to substantially reshuffle unemployment. In a country like Japan where young workers are cheap relative to older workers, unemployment is concentrated among those 55 to 65 years of age and not among the young. And with a different wage structure it would not be concentrated among the young here either.

Wage subsidies are also preferable to the current strategy of creating millions of public-service jobs to lower the unemployment of economic minorities. While there is a role for public-service employment in improving the background characteristics (work habits, literacy, and such) of disadvantaged workers, they are not a good substitute for regular jobs. Since they do not eliminate the relative scarcity of prime-age white males in the regular economy, they do not permit an increase in macroeconomic stimulation. They do not provide the lifetime career opportunities and salable skills that are created by regular jobs. Public-service employment at the minimum wage (the current plan) does little to help achieve income parity. And as the public-service jobs programs are currently structured, no person is to hold a job for more than one year. What do they do then?

In the end the only choice is between living with the current stagflation and lack of economic integration (including the gradual growth of millions of public-service jobs) or using wage subsidies to reshuffle unemployment in conjunction with monetary and fiscal policies to lower aggregate unemployment. It would be nice to have a better choice, but there is none.

VI. Reducing the Rate of Inflation

Given a heavily indexed economy subject to occasional upward price shocks caused by events (Iranian oil cutoffs, an adverse meat cycle, and such) and policies (Social Security tax increases, steel reference pricing, and such), there are essentially three options for reducing inflation. Each of them has severe drawbacks. In each case the cure may be worse than the disease.

(1) Monetary and fiscal policies could be used to create a recession large enough to crack inflationary expectations and indexing. (2) Wage-and-price controls could be used to reduce the rate of inflation. And (3) microeconomic policies could be used on a sector-by-sector basis to reduce prices wherever possible.

While no one doubts that there is some level of unemployment which would crack inflationary expectations and drive cost-of-living escalator clauses out of the economy, no one knows exactly how high unemployment would have to be. One would certainly have to contemplate something in excess of 10 percent for an extended period of time. Given that each percentage point of unemployment represents approximately $75 billion annually in lost output, the economic costs of fighting inflation with a recession are obviously high. In addition the costs would not be evenly shared. The inflation fighters (the unemployed) would be heavily recruited from among minorities, women, and the young—precisely the groups that now suffer from very high unemployment. There is also a real question as to whether the political process could tolerate an extended period of deliberately induced massive unemployment.

The second option is to adopt some kind of an incomes policy. What an incomes policy has to do is clear. Assume an indexed economy with an 8 percent rate of inflation. If everyone agreed to raise his or her wages or prices by only 5 percent instead of the specified 8 percent, no one would be worse off and the inflation rate would be reduced to 5 percent. In the next round it could be reduced to 3 percent and so on. How to accomplish this, however, is not clear. Every individual economic actor has an incentive to raise his wage or price by the full 8 percent. If this is done and the rest of the world goes down to a 5 percent gain, he or she will have increased their real income by 3 percent. Conversely, if they cooperate with the incomes policy and go down to a 5 percent gain while everyone else stays at 8 percent, they will have made a 3 percent income loss. Thus there is no such thing as a voluntary incomes policy. The incentives not to cooperate are simply too large.

The currently fashionable form of incomes policy discussion revolves around a "tax-based incomes policy." Employers would be given a series of tax incentives or penalties, depending on whether they did or did not live up to some enunciated standard of noninflationary behavior. A tax-based incomes policy is, however, just equivalent to a set of ,wage-and-price controls with a predetermined set of financial penalties for violators. Catching the violators and enforcing the rules is no less difficult or expensive. The system is more flexible (if you want to violate the rules you can pay your penalty and violate the rules), but it is every bit as complex and expensive to administer. Detailed norms must be written and then enforced. In World War II 400,000 price-and-wage inspectors were necessary to make the system work. There have been advances in computational techniques, but the economy is now much larger than it was then. Any serious system would undoubtedly require an equal number of employees. There is no such thing as wage-and-price controls without a large bureaucracy to administer them.

There is also a real question as to whether any compulsory incomes policy is possible in a democratic peacetime economy. Even with 400,000 price inspectors the system needs widespread voluntary cooperation. Without some external threat it is difficult to envision the necessary degree of voluntary cooperation.

The third strategy is to use government policies to jolt the economy with a series of negative price shocks that will become embedded in the structure of indexing and thus carried into the future as a permanently lowered rate of inflation. The current deregulation of the airlines industry (and the resultant reduction in air fares) is one such program. If we can lower air-transportation costs, this lowers the measured rate of inflation. With a lower inflation rate and indexing, all wages and prices will go up less than they otherwise would have, and the future rate of inflation is less than it otherwise would have been. The same thing could be done in trucking. Instead of raising Social Security taxes (a tax which shows up in the cost-of-living index) and cutting income tax (a tax that does not show up in the cost of living), all tax cuts should be focused on those taxes which reduce the cost of living, and all tax increases should be focused on those taxes that do not show up in the cost of living.

There are a host of government programs designed to raise prices that could be abandoned. Such programs now exist in agriculture, the maritime industry, the steel industry, textiles, shoes, and a number of others. Abandoning any or all of these programs would reduce the measured rate of inflation. The postal service could be made subject to private competition.

While the economics of the third antiinflationary strategy is clear, the politics are not clear. Each of these antiinflationary actions has a vigorous set of opponents. The airlines and truckers do not want transportation deregulated. Upper-income groups would rather have income-tax reductions than sales-tax reductions. State and local governments want their grants-in-aid without strings. Each of the industries protected by government policies to raise prices wants these policies kept in place.

Everyone is in favor of reducing the rate of inflation as long as this is accomplished by lowering someone else's income, but everyone is also against any antiinflationary policy that lowers his or her income. Unfortunately an effective antiinflationary policy has to lower someone's income below what it otherwise would be. This is not a matter of economic analysis but simply an algebraic truism. Whose income is going to be the first to go down?

VII. Productivity as a "Cure-All"

Historically, accelerating the rate of growth of productivity seems to fall within the focus of public policy about once every decade. In the 1950s it was seen as a policy for keeping the U.S. ahead of the USSR economically. In the 1960s it was seen as both a threat to and an opportunity for economic progress of minority groups and the poor. In the late 1970s it is seen as a painless cure to inflation. If, and this is a big "if," productivity rose and money wages remained the same, the rate of inflation would fall. If the rate of growth of productivity could be accelerated, the value of the dollar would not fall as much as it otherwise would.

Accelerating the rate of growth of productivity is often seen as a simple four-part task: (1) Raise expenditures on research and development: (2) Raise expenditures on plant and equipment: (3) Raise investment in human capital skill acquisition: And (4) remove market imperfections that stop the economy from being as efficient as it might be.

The third and fourth tasks impact the labor market,

but their implementation differs radically depending upon whether you believe the four neoclassical hypotheses or the four alternatives that I have been suggesting. From the neoclassical perspective you simply invest more in educating and training the labor force and take actions wherever possible to promote wage flexibility. Any monopoly elements (unions, minimum wages, and such) are to be removed. From the perspective of the four alternative hypotheses the problem is more complex.

Since skills are acquired on the job, it is necessary to generate a structure of new job opportunties that will lead to more skill acquisition. Simple wage flexibility is counterproductive if it disrupts production and training. Instead, job guarantees must be structured in such a way that technical progress becomes nonthreatening to those who are participating in it. More efforts must be made to generate team productivity and a faster descent down the learning curves.

But before we look at this strategy in detail, let us first see what lessons can explain the downturn in productivity in the 1970s. Perhaps they can shed light on those factors which might accelerate the rate of growth and productivity.

From 1947 to 1970 output per man-hour rose at 3.1 percent in the private economy.[7] From 1970 to 1977 it rose at 1.8 percent per year. What factors could explain this downturn? Investment in research and development (R&D) fell from 3 percent of the GNP in the late 1970s, but the time lags between investment in R&D and its impact on the economy are so long that this reduction cannot explain the current problem. Productivity turned down before R&D expenditures turned down. A lack of R&D in the late 1970s will affect productivity in the mid-1980s but not before that time.

The downturn also cannot be traced to a lack of

investment in plant and equipment investment. From 1947 to 1970 plant and equipment investment averaged 9.8 percent of GNP, but from 1970 to 1977 it averaged 10.1 percent of GNP. Plant and equipment investment is up, not down.

Much of the source of the problem can be seen in a disaggregate view of where productivity is growing and where productivity is not growing. Manufacturing productivity, for example, is not down. It grew at 2.8 percent per year in the 1947–70 period and 2.8 percent per year in the 1970–77 period. Whatever the problem, it does not lie in the realm of manufacturing. And it is precisely in this sector that one would expect to find the largest effects if the downturn were due to safety or pollution regulations and investments.

Farm productivity is down from 5.9 percent per year to 4.4 percent per year between the two periods, but this is not a subject for worry or even evidence of a decline in the rate of growth of agricultural productivity. All of this decrease in the rate of growth of productivity can be traced to the reabsorption of millions of low productivity acres that were brought back into production with the dismantling of acreage controls in 1973–74. Once this shift is factored into the analysis, there is no evidence of a decrease in agricultural productivity.

As a result, whatever the problems, they must exist in the nonfarm, nonmanufacturing sector of the economy. And here productivity has in fact fallen from 2.3 to 1.2 percent per year. A small part of this decline can be traced to pollution and health or safety regulations. With the advent of these regulations output per full-time equivalent worker has fallen 19 percent in mining and 6 percent in construction. A much larger part, however, can be traced to an adverse shift in the growth in demand for goods and services. From 1970 to 1977 the private economy added 8.6 million new workers. Most of these workers were, however, added in two low-productivity sectors of the economy. Retail trade expanded its employment by 3.2 million, but retail trade has a level of productivity which is 35 percent below the national average. Another 3.7 million workers were added in the service industries, but this industry also had a level of productivity 35 percent below the national average. If we look within services, almost half of those 3.7 million people were added to the health-care service industries. If demand expands so that 6.9 million out of 8.6 million new jobs are created in industries with productivity far below the national average, it is not surprising that the overall rate of growth of productivity slows down.

Conversely, if you want to accelerate the rate of growth of productivity, it is necessary to organize the economy so that demands grow in high-productivity industries and fall in low-productivity industries. Control of health-care costs is a key ingredient not only in the cost of living and in balancing government budgets but in raising the rate of growth of productivity. If we double the percentage of the GNP devoted to health, as we have in the past two decades, we freeze ourselves into a structure of low productivity.

If one wants to accelerate the rate of growth of productivity, getting out of low-productivity industries is just as important as getting into high-productivity industries. Disinvestment is just as important as investment. Regulations which protect an inefficient domestic steel industry or an inefficient domestic textile industry are actions which lead to a low rate of growth of productivity.

But given an adequate structure of demand, what changes should take place on the employment side of the equation? What promotes efficiency when skills are endogenously acquired on the job, marginal products are individually variable, preferences are interdependent, and team productivity is an important element of total productivity?

R&D expenditures and plant and equipment (P&E) investment are certainly necessary to generate new jobs and the need for new or expanded skills. It is not possible to expand exogenously the real working skills of the labor force by expanding formal education or training. But R&D expenditures and P&E investment will not lead to the desired results unless they are accompanied by something else. This something else can be seen in the famous learning curve (see diagram 1).

New plants and processes typically exhibit a sharp increase in productivity as they swing into operation. This gain in productivity is a mystery from the point of view of neoclassical labor economics but easily understandable from the point of view of the alternative hypotheses. It reflects an on-the-job learning process as

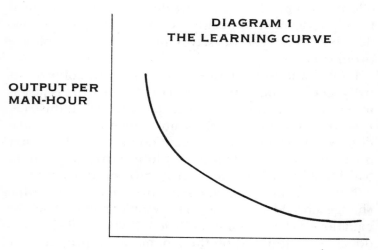

DIAGRAM 1
THE LEARNING CURVE

OUTPUT PER
MAN-HOUR

t

workers acquire new skills or polish the precise skills that they need in the new plant or process. In addition, teamwork emerges as any group of workers learns to work together. This acquisition of individual skills and teamwork typically lowers man-hours per unit of output drastically. New investments are profitable or unprofitable depending upon the steepness of the learning curve. To raise the rate of growth of productivity, the learning curve must be steepened and lowered.[8]

Since teamwork depends upon having a period of time to work together, some simulations indicate that a 40 percent increase in productivity could be obtained if labor-force turnover could be lowered from 3 percent to 1 percent per month. Actual turnover in U.S. manufacturing is near 4 percent per month.

From this point of view, it is important to operate fiscal and monetary policies in such a way that they encourage the construction of new plants rather than the modification of old plants. Learning curves can be steep only when there are real opportunities for learning to occur. High interest rates which lead to very short time horizons can be counterproductive with respect to the long-run rate of growth of productivity and hence the long-run rate of inflation.

While foreign analogies should always be treated with caution, it is instructive to think about the Japanese labor market and Japan's high rate of growth of productivity. Imagine what a neoclassical labor economist would predict about the rate of growth of productivity in an economy where many workers are given lifetime jobs and where wage increases depend almost entirely on seniority rather than merit. Yet the Japanese have the highest rate of growth of productivity of all the industrialized countries. Why?

I think there are a number of reasons. With lifetime

employment and seniority wages technical progress is
not threatening. It is not going to lead to unemployment
or wage reductions. When combined with another factor
in the Japanese labor market, it is in fact beneficial. Since
the typical worker gets about 50 percent of his or her
wages in a twice-yearly bonus that is based on profits,
every worker has an incentive to maximize productivity,
acquire individual skills, and contribute to the industrial
team. In the short run only an increase in productivity
can raise their own income.

Steep, low-earning curves are in the self-interest of
each worker. The result is a situation where the Japanese
seem to be able to operate identical plants at a higher
level of productivity than their competitors. They make
the same investment but get a higher return. Let me
suggest that this higher return is related to the structure
of their labor market. It is a labor-market structure not to
take advantage of the neoclassical postulates but a
labor-market structure to maximize productivity in the
presence of the alternative hypotheses.

While cultures are certainly different, the Japanese
model should give us pause. If we could wave a magic
wand and create wage flexibility, would we want to do so?
Wage flexibility would put us on the efficiency frontier
(move us from A to B), but what if the disruption caused
by wage flexibility slows the rate of growth of the efficiency frontier (see diagram 2)? In anything but the
very short run there is much more to be gained by
moving the frontier to the right than there is to be gained
by moving from A to B.

As a result, I would argue that the rigid wages and
seniority hiring and firing that we started out examining
are, not marks of efficiency or market imperfections, but
basic ingredients in promoting growth. They exist because they are functional. If they were nonfunctional,
they long ago would have disappeared from the scene.

VIII. Conclusions

Endogenous skills, variable marginal products, interdependent preferences, team productivity—such a world is not a simple world where we can deductively assert what is true and false, what is efficient and inefficient. Yet in many ways it is a more interesting world. If the neoclassical hypotheses were actually to exist, there would be little for a labor economist to say or do. With 100 percent market efficiency there would be no need for economists.

As a teacher in both a department of economics and a business school, I am always intrigued by the different assumptions about efficiency. Economics departments often teach courses as if business decisions were 100 percent efficient or as close to that as it is possible to get. Business schools usually teach their courses as if there were a large gap between actual and potential efficiency. If the gap did not exist, there would, after all, be no role for business schools. Reality is more complex than simple competitive assumptions admit.

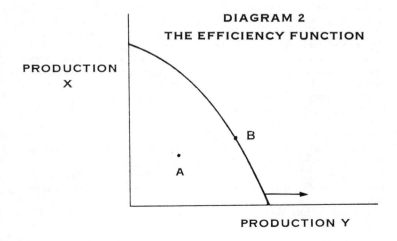

DIAGRAM 2
THE EFFICIENCY FUNCTION

PRODUCTION X

PRODUCTION Y

NOTES

1. U.S. Department of Labor, *Formal Occupational Training of Adult Workers,* Manpower Automation Research Monograph, no. 2 (Washington D.C.: Government Printing Office, 1964), pp. 3, 18, 20, 43.

2. Richard Esterlin, "Does Money Buy Happiness?" *The Public Interest* 30 (winter 1973): 3–10.

3. Lester C. Thurow and Stephen Sheffrin, "Measuring the Costs and Benefits of On-the-Job Training," *Economie Appliquée* 3 (1977).

4. The quintile cost-of-living indexes were calculated in the following manner: First, consumption was divided into 13 different categories (food, clothing, etc.) for which both implicit price deflators and expenditure data by income class were available. The implicit price deflators were taken from the *Survey of Current Business* and the expenditure data by income class were taken from the most recent *Survey of Consumer Expenditures* (1973–74). Using the expenditure patterns for the mean income of each quintile and the 1972–77 change in deflators for each of the 13 expenditure categories, it is a simple matter of algebraic calculations to calculate a price index for each of the five quintiles. Since the average index calculated in this manner will differ slightly from the aggregate implicit price deflator for personal consumption expenditures for the 1972–77 period, the results were then scaled to make them compatible with the actual implicit price deflator for personal consumption expenditures.

5. The asset classes found in the IRS data are negative debts and mortgages, cash, corporate stock, corporate and government bonds, life insurance equity, notes and mortgages, real estate, noncorporate business assets, and other assets. In each case the procedure was to inflate the 1972 amount of each of these asset types by the amount that that type of asset had gone up or down in the period from 1972 to 1977. In some cases it was not possible to find the exact analogue in aggregate data. In these cases an attempt was made to find an equivalent economic analogue. Thus, the value of noncorporate assets was assumed to have gone up by the same amount as noncorporate profits. The relevant percent: cash up 88.6 percent, corporate stocks down 10.9 percent, bonds up 77.9 percent, notes and mortgages up 63.8 percent, real estate up 53.5 percent, life insurance equity up 46.2 percent, noncorporate business assets up 32.0 percent, and other assets up 63.4 percent.

6. Congressional Budget Office, *Policy Options for the Teenage Unemployment Problem.* Paper 13, September 21, 1976.

7. Additional data in this section are taken from the National Income and Product Accounts, *Survey of Current Business,* various issues.

8. Thurow and Sheffrin, "Measuring the Costs and Benefits."

The Decline of Union Bargaining Power

Charles Craypo

I. Introduction

DURING THE WORLD WAR II era a number of American economists, contemplating the social significance of the recent surge of industrial unionism in this country, raised the specter of unrestrained union monopoly power. Economists of liberal as well as conservative persuasion joined the issue. From Chicago Henry Simons sketched a scenario in which "militant labor monopolies," meaning trade unions, acquire destructive control over industrial activity through their potential or actual strike action. Pursuing a "natural function" of exploitation, unions precipitate widespread disruption and distortion of economic markets and in time bring the economy to ruin. Overwhelming social forces are unleashed in the aftermath; the Republic sinks into chaos and, ultimately, succumbs to political dictatorship, similar to what Simons' generation had witnessed in prewar Germany and Italy.[1]

Writing from a position friendlier to organized labor, Charles Lindblom nevertheless accepted the incompatibility of unions and free markets and the proposition that unionized labor's economic power invariably exceeds that of capital. Unions being political organizations, union leaders cannot be expected reasonably to be "responsible." Government must therefore preserve the market system against excessive wage demands of monopoly labor if capital is to perform its prescribed role in the free economy.[2]

Such apprehensions never materialized. Aside from some rather well-publicized pockets of pervasive union bargaining strength, organized labor has not attained the power attributed to it by these and other writers. Indeed, the American labor movement today resembles more the movement of the 1920s, the nadir of evolutionary unionism in this country, than that of the 1930s and 1940s. The institutional and environmental parallels with the 20s are striking. In both periods organized labor is characterized by (1) declining ratios of union and nonunion workers, (2) aged and uninspiring leadership, (3) organizational structures made obsolete by changing capital formations, (4) inability to secure passage of favorable legislation, (5) failure to stop technological erosion of unionized work groups, (6) ineffectiveness against imaginative, aggressive employer attacks upon established bargaining units, and (7) loss of power in a host of industries in which unions previously had enjoyed considerable bargaining leverage.

This paper describes and analyses the last: the decline of union bargaining power in a variety of industries. First, the market and institutional conditions necessary for union bargaining strength are identified and explained. Second, a number of current bargaining situations in both primary and secondary industries are described to show the nature and extent of declining union power. Third, alternative union policy responses are identified and briefly assessed.

II. The Sources of Union Bargaining Strength

Five market and institutional conditions are crucial to establishing and maintaining union bargaining power. Two of them determine the employer's ability to pay higher labor costs; three determine the union's ability to make the employer pay. Together they distinguish strong from weak unions.

Industrial employers have greater ability to pay higher labor costs where (1) product market conditions permit them to pass on such costs in the form of higher product prices without jeopardizing their sales revenues or where (2) technical production methods enable them to offset higher money costs for labor with productivity increases. Either condition alone may be sufficient theoretically to establish the industry's ability to pay higher labor costs. But in practice above-average productivity gains often accompany the structural characteristics associated with seller power in product markets.

Three types of industrial structure enable employers to pass on higher labor costs in product markets: (a) concentrated industries in which administered-pricing practices prevail; (b) government-regulated industries in which higher labor costs are routinely incorporated into user rates; (c) geographically constrained industries in which "spatial monopolies" permit uniform increases in labor costs despite price competition among firms in product markets.

Concentrated manufacturing industries show an ability to recoup higher labor costs through higher product prices. Years ago, for example, the research department of the United Auto Workers union calculated that in the decade following World War II General Motors obtained $3.75 in added revenue from price increases for every additional $1 in wages it paid to UAW members as a result of negotiated increases; the comparable figure for Ford was $5.[3] Structural and behavioral patterns typifying such oligopolized industries support the proposition they have discretionary price capabilities.[4]

Government-regulated industries, whether concentrated or not, normally are allowed to pass through higher labor costs. This certainly has been the case, for example, in interstate trucking, railroads, telecommunications, airlines, and power utilities.[5]

Without either organizational concentration or regulatory rate-setting or both, another group of industries is nevertheless able to pass on higher labor costs. This includes those industries where the work can be performed only at a finite number of locations or for a limited number of employers. If, for example, the workers in a particular building-trades craft, say plumbing and pipefitting, stay within a specified labor-market area and belong to the local plumbers union, the latter has a "spatial monopoly" in its negotiations with area contractors. This is because commercial and residential structures cannot be built in one place and located in another, and further because plumbing and pipefitting skills are essential to the construction process. With the available work force securely in hand, the union can negotiate higher labor costs that must in the end be paid by the buyer of the building. Barring the development of prefabricated structures or other suitable substitutes for on-site production or the introduction of labor-displacing technology, the union can hike wage-and-benefit costs to the extent it feels necessary or justified, provided of course it keeps nonunion workers out of its jurisdiction. Conceptually, the same potential exists for "spatial monopoly" situations in printing and longshoring, among other industries.[6]

In order to make the employer pay higher labor costs, unions must establish three conditions. First, it has to organize the relevant work force. That includes all workers performing production tasks. In other words, unions must follow the work. How far they follow it depends on the product. Products manufactured and marketed nationally must be made under union conditions regardless of the number and locations of plants if the union wishes to have bargaining strength. Employer ability to assemble automobiles, make tons of steel, or knit fabric beyond the reach of union contracts undermines established standards and conditions. Widespread movement of domestic textile production from northern to southern states before and following World War II is a classic example of the threat posed to unionized sectors by nonunion workers in national product markets. Industrial unionists are acutely aware of the problem. Perceptively, the UAW is following the movement of General Motors parts production facilities to southern states, not resting until it wins union certifications in each new plant.

Where products and services are intended for local markets, the relevant work occurs at that level. Here organization occurs frequently along occupational rather than product lines, as in the spatial monopoly situation. For this reason much of organized labor's structural evolution in the face of changing capital formations can be seen in terms of a simple dichotomy. The older organizations are named after occupations, denoting the fact that employers then were users of skilled labor in localized industry; the younger, industrial unions, by contrast, are named after products, reflecting the fact the employers they organized used mostly unskilled and semiskilled workers in national, mass-production industries.

The second structural requirement for labor bargaining power is elimination of competitive unionism. Where more unions than one negotiate independently with employers for some or all of their employees, the unions are vulnerable to whipsaw tactics in which one is played off against the others. Industry examples of such tactical bargaining disadvantage by U.S. unions in recent years are electrical products, nonferrous metal mining and smelting, chemicals, and oil refining. In some instances the unions involved established coordinated bargaining councils in an effort to reconcile their differences and present a united front against the employers. The most highly publicized such assault was against General Electric. By the mid-1960s interindustry wage-and-benefit standards for the electrical-products industry had deteriorated dramatically following GE's decision in the early 1950s to adopt a hard-line bargaining posture. Its strategy rested on direct employer-employee labor relations—circumventing certified unions as much as possible—and "take-it-or-leave-it" contract renegotiations.[7] This behavior was later ruled illegal by the Supreme Court, but in the meantime more than a dozen previously competing international unions had organized coordinated bargaining committees for each of the major electrical companies; after lengthy but successful strikes the cooperating unions began to reverse the unfavorable economic trend.

A third requirement of union bargaining strength is sufficient centralization of the bargaining structure to ensure that the economic terms and conditions of the relevant work force are negotiated in a single agreement, or, if more than one agreement is negotiated, that their economic provisions be identical or nearly so. A predictably strong, though informal, pattern of settlements among partially centralized bargaining structures, as in the pulp and paper industry, normally will suffice in this regard. In any event, once accomplished, a consolidated bargaining structure effectively takes relevant work-force wages out of competition. Taking wages out of competition is the historic mission of labor movements in the market economy. As earlier discussion suggests, the union's preferred bargaining structure differs depending on industry organization and the production processes. A contract covering all the skilled tradesmen in a specific labor-market area is sufficient in craft settings, and one including all shipping ports on the Pacific Coast is adequate in longshoring, but one that includes not one or a few but all the primary aluminum mills and fabricating plants is necessary in that industry.

A moment's reflection will confirm that America's more successful labor unions are those that have attained sufficient centralization of their bargaining structures. This would include, among other industries, railroads, interstate trucking, certain areawide building and construction trades, and of course such industrial union bastions as auto and steel. A striking example of the importance of bargaining structure in determining union strength occurs in the intercity bus industry. The Amalgamated Transit Union's national bargaining unit in Greyhound enables it to negotiate large economic differentials above the fragmented contracts it and another union negotiate for more than a dozen bargaining units in Trailways.[8]

III. Sources of Declining Union Bargaining Power

Once attained, union bargaining power is by no means a continued certainty. It is often transient. Even if a union which represents workers in an industry that has the ability to pay high wages and benefits does establish the structural conditions prerequisite to the union's ability to deliver benefits, there is the prospect that over time changed conditions may erode its established bargaining position. Each of three types of change is capable of doing this: (1) industrial organization, (2) technology, and (3) public policy.

Horizontal, vertical, or diversified consolidation of corporate structures can diminish existing union bargaining strength by changing the composition of the relevant work force. Unless the union can make corresponding changes in its organizational coverage and bargaining structure it is in jeopardy of being outflanked by nonunion production sources. Probably the most interesting historical example is the Amalgamated Association's desperate strike in 1901 against the newly formed U.S. Steel trust. Prior to steel's consolidation, the Amalgamated, a narrow but militant craft union, had considerable organization strength in certain independent steel firms, some of them multimill operations. But nine years earlier it had been hurt in a confrontation at Andrew Carnegie's largest mill. Horizontal and vertical integration dismantled the union's bargaining structure by throwing together union and nonunion facilities. Having little choice in the matter, the union demanded corporatewide recognition; when the owners demurred, because they feared the effects of a major labor dispute so soon after U.S. Steel's organization, the union struck, first the principal fabricating mills and eventually all the basic steel operations. Despite a surprising show of solidarity by workers in previously unorganized mills, the strike was lost after a few months. Never again was Amalgamated a force in the industry.[9]

Changing industrial technology usually undermines union bargaining power. It does so by destroying the skill-based bargaining leverage of the traditional relevant work force as employers find they can substitute machinery or unskilled labor. By contrast, it can be said of the earlier technology of mass production that it created jobs. Product standardization combined with extreme division of labor lowered unit production costs; product prices fell to generally affordable levels, widening markets and requiring large numbers of unskilled and semiskilled workers. In this way technology fostered the emergence of industrial unionism in America.

Present technology tends in the opposite direction, however. Often it eliminates entirely the previous need for specific occupations in a production process. In other instances it reconstitutes jobs to move the work out of an existing union bargaining unit. Either change erodes union power. New technology creates new jobs, of course, but not within the same context of union control as those eliminated. Union power depends, not on the total pool of jobs, but on the proportion of them being worked under strong contracts.

Public policy, the third area of possible change, shapes the institutional environment within which unions function. Union organizing and bargaining success rests considerably on the ground rules set out by legislative, judicial, and administrative bodies. While it has not always been so, today public policy on balance probably works against union bargaining power. The apex of procollective bargaining policy in this country occurred in the mid-1930s, with passage of the Wagner Act coinciding with a peak in public sympathy for unions. This legislation followed a history of antiunion, court-made labor policy. Union organization rights, bargaining-agent certification, and good-faith bargaining requirements facilitated massive organizing drives and subsequent negotiation of comprehensive industrywide, companywide, and multiplant contracts. Major revisions of the act in 1947 and 1959 imposed several restrictions on union organizing and bargaining tactics, reflecting an evident shift in public opinion. Unions were believed to have become powerful, corrupt, and undemocratic. More important for this analysis are the philosophy and present administration of the law. The National Labor Relations Act (the amended Wagner Act) is remedial rather than punitive in intent, meaning that in specific disputes it is the purpose of the law to remedy the effect of an illegal action by restoring the union-management relation prior to any violation. Penalties under the law are tempered accordingly.

Remedial justice presumes there is a mutual acceptance by the parties of each other's institutional presence and a spirit of honest difference. But if one or both of them treat the law as part of their overall labor-relations strategy aimed at acquiring or preserving tactical power, then this remedial intent undermines the law's effectiveness. Calculated observance or violation of labor law occurs in a cost-benefit framework where the cost is consistently low. Nothing has happened to the J. P. Stevens Company, to cite the best-publicized case to date, as a result of its more than two dozen convictions for labor-law violations — many of them remarkably flagrant in nature — to deter that firm from its determination to operate union-free. The costs incurred so far in back-pay awards to J. P. Stevens millhands who were fired for their union sympathies and activities are as nothing compared to the inestimable benefits of years of not having to observe the terms and conditions of union contracts.[10]

An additional policy source of declining union bargaining power involves labor-law administration. The National Labor Relations Board, which enforces the act, has so far taken an inflexible position on the important

4

matter of appropriate bargaining units. Changes in corporate structure or technology can suddenly make obsolete an existing bargaining structure, leaving the union without leverage. New structures can be organized only by mutual agreement of the parties or labor board order. But the board refuses to restructure existing units in response to environmental changes. A certain institutional rigidity in making decisions that involve a delicate balancing of opposing interest is understandable. But the effect here is to freeze legal bargaining relationships that have their logical origins in another era.

IV. Trends in Relative Union-Industry Bargaining Power

A survey of recent bargaining events shows instances of loss of union bargaining power due to changes in organization, technology, and policy in three industrial sectors:

(1) primary manufacturing, service, and mining;
(2) basic manufacturing supply and fabricating;
(3) secondary manufacturing and service.

Collective bargaining in America has been reasonably stable since the turbulence in labor-capital relations of the 1930s. In large part this stability was made possible by steady postwar gains in real national output, advances which allowed unions and managers to negotiate larger and larger real incomes for workers. Today, however, many industries are undergoing fundamental changes in structure, technology, and market environment. The frictions associated with these changes often result in escalating levels of union-management confrontation.

Primary Manufacturing, Nonmanufacturing, and Mining

Primary, or basic, industry, so-defined here because of its importance to the economy and its sizable work force, has been a bastion of industrial union power. But now a number of these industries are experiencing the kind of changes that weaken an incumbent union's position. Examples include meatpacking and meatcutting, tires and tubes, bituminous coal, chemicals, newspapers, and some portions of the building and construction trades. Of greater significance perhaps is the potential for similar changes in a broader range of industries besides these.

Meatpacking and Meatcutting. Meatpacking and meatcutting are among the historically high-wage, high-benefit industrial and craft occupations. Meatpacking was well-organized nationally, though by two rival unions, the Packinghouse Workers, a CIO union, and the Amalgamated Meat Cutters, an AFL affiliate. Each had master contracts with separate national packers, resulting in a system of pattern bargaining in the industry. Since 1950 labor relations have been relatively conflict-free among the Big Four companies: Swift, Wilson, Armour, and Cudahy.[11] Retail meatcutting, which was the exclusive jurisdiction of the Meat Cutters, by contrast was not solidly unionized nationally. Its spatial monopoly character and skilled labor requirements nevertheless enabled the union to negotiate strong contracts with the industry's well-unionized northern and urban chain food stores.

Geographic decentralization of operations and technological changes caused job losses in meatpacking throughout the 1960s and prompted a 1968 merger of the two unions in which the Meat Cutters was the surviving organization. No sooner had this been accomplished, and the traditional rivalry between the two organizations eliminated, than corporate reorganization and new technology combined to undermine the Meat Cutters' tactical bargaining position in both meatpacking and meatcutting.

Structurally each of the Big Four meatpackers was acquired by conglomerate firms. While this change did not alter existing bargaining structures, it meant the union now negotiated with subsidiaries of larger, more complex, and financially powerful companies. Corporate objectives and decision-making processes were less clear to the union, and in the event of a strike there was always the possibility of intracorporate financing of the meatpacking operations by the parent firm's other divisions.

More important to the loss of union leverage was the rise of Iowa Beef Processors. Through vigorous acquisition of existing companies, innovative processing methods, and aggressive marketing practices, within a decade Iowa Beef emerged from the middle ranks of the industry to become the nation's largest packer. It completely reshaped industry production, sales, and labor relations.

Its success invited imitation. MBPXL, the product of a 1974 merger of two large independent packers, was inspired to duplicate on a smaller scale Iowa Beef's policies, as have two or three other new entrants in the industry. Reversing the trend toward fragmentation, Iowa Beef concentrated its operations in huge vertically integrated facilities where animals are slaughtered and fabricated into various product lines. Meat products are processed and then boxed for refrigerated rail shipment and direct sale to wholesale users and retail sellers. Boxing of meat cuts also eliminates skilled cutting in sales-market areas. As a result, the major packing firms

have established standardized cutting centers in metropolitan areas that use mostly unskilled hourly labor to do
the cutting. The combined effect of these trends is to
shrink the number of meat-cutter jobs in retail markets
and reduce the union's bargaining position.

At the meatpacking stages of production Iowa Beef
has fragmented union bargaining strength. Union representation at its large western plants is divided between
the Meat Cutters, which has two facilities, and the Teamsters, with one plant, while four others are nonunion.
Wages and benefits negotiated by the Teamsters are
much below those at Meat Cutter plants in both Iowa
Beef and MBPXL.[12] Standards in the Big Four, which
negotiate almost exclusively with the Meat Cutters, are in
turn also considerably higher than in all of Iowa Beef's
plants. These differentials put the Meat Cutters in the
unhappy position of inviting the resistance of the conglomerate owners of the Big Four firms against any
wage-and-benefit demands that will further increase
their labor costs relative to those of Iowa Beef and its
imitators. On the other hand, the union is unable to force
economic concessions from Iowa Beef that would narrow
the gap.

Conflict, sometimes violent, has characterized labor
relations between Iowa Beef and the Meat Cutters.
Strikes at one or both plants have occurred in each round
of bargaining since 1969. In 1977–78 the union struck
one of them fourteen months in an unsuccessful attempt
to reduce these wage-and-benefit differentials, which the
union claims then ranged as high as $2.90 per hour.[13]
The final settlement provided for wages equal to those
Iowa Beef had been paying strikebreakers at the plant
for five months.

That outcome sets the stage for possible future conflict
between the Meat Cutters and Big Four negotiators over

efforts by the latter to contain union contract demands in order to prevent further widening of the differential in labor costs with Iowa Beef and MBPXL. Meanwhile, further consolidation has taken place in both the industry and the union. MBPXL was acquired by a large diversified firm. Then in 1979 the Meat Cutters merged with the Retail Clerks union to form the biggest AFL-CIO affiliate. Meat Cutters officers attributed the consolidation to labor's need to combine in the face of corporate integration. "Conglomerates in the meat packing industry are the order of the day and corporate power is almost unregulated," noted the union's president.[14]

Rubber Tires. Wages and fringe benefits in tires and tubes are high. But in recent years underlying structural changes in the industry have eroded the bargaining position of the United Rubber Workers (URW). Truck and auto tire production has been moved south and overseas, major tire producers have divested and shut down nontire rubber products plants, technology has encouraged plant relocation outside the union's geographical power base, and, finally, a large, foreign-based multinational tire maker has established extensive but nonunion production capabilities in this country.

Together these trends deprive the URW of its historic organization of the relevant work force and its moderately concentrated bargaining structure and strong wage-and-benefit pattern in the tire industry. The tire pattern had been extended to nontire products. But lately the union is losing its capacity to inflict serious strike damage on the major domestic rubber companies. Despite a history of militant strike action by the workers in tires, production workers in the industry have been losing ground in their negotiated economic standards to workers in more stable basic manufacturing industries.[15] This is not due to any leadership failure or membership irresolution, but rather the determining structural conditions are simply turning against them. In 1968 average hourly earnings in tires and tubes ranked second only to brewing among manufacturing industries, whereas today at least seven other industries rank higher. While wage differences are not definitive indicators of comparative union bargaining effectiveness, they do provide some indication of the relative rise and fall of individual union strength.

Although it is highly concentrated both horizontally and vertically, the tire-and-tube industry has not been as profitable as other, equally concentrated industries. This lesser control over product markets is a result of the countervailing power of volume buyers — auto manufacturers and national retail chains. Tire producers have customarily had to given them 30–40 percent price discounts, which explains the concentration of tire industry profits among the Big Four firms (Goodyear, Firestone, Goodrich, Uniroyal). Marginal manufacturers do not have sufficient economies of production to offset such revenue concessions.[16]

Contract negotiations in tires, tubes, and nontire rubber products has centered upon the economic settlement reached between URW and one of the Big Four's Akron plants. That agreement becomes the pattern for the other large producers in Akron and elsewhere as well as for the smaller companies. Until recently most of the industry's productive capacity has been organized; much of it was located in Akron or other northeast manufacturing centers. Under these circumstances strikes were effective. Stoppages called against a target company put that firm at a relative disadvantage and prompted settlement on terms favorable to the union, a tactical situation the employers tried to counter with their own mutual strike-aid pact. The union would then try to extend its basic tire settlement to the nontire rubber plants of the Big Four. While it seldom matched fully the tire pattern in these plants, the union kept them close to the basic contracts. It usually succeeded in extending outward new fringe benefits won in tires.

Today, however, as a result of massive production relocation, no tires are made in Akron. Moreover, the U.S. is now the largest importer of tires in the world. And each of the Big Four firms has nonunion plants in the south. Five of Firestone's ten tire plants were not covered by the URW's master contract during the lengthy 1976 industrywide strike; General Tire, the fifth-largest tire company, remained unaffected by the stoppage because local union officials chose not to strike; Michelin's South Carolina tire-production complex operated nonunion; Goodyear's Kelly-Springfield and other tire subsidiaries also stayed outside the strike. Something slightly more than one-half the total domestic tire production was affected by the strike, a situation preventing the URW from achieving its declared objective of stopping domestic auto production by depriving auto assembly plants of tires. After a six-month walkout the union went back to work for a substantial money settlement without having won the job protections it demanded and with a cleavage having been made in the traditional inclusion of key nontire plants in the pattern.[17]

Changing technology also damaged the union's bargaining position. Faster and bigger machines combined with mechanized materials-handling and automated-control instrumentation had made the northern plants expendable. Machine operators in newer, nonunion southern plants worked at three times the productivity levels of the older plants. Thousands of production jobs disappeared throughout the industry. During 1960–72 the ratio of capital expenditures to production increased 7 percent annually while payroll costs relative to production decreased 1.6 percent yearly.

Three years after the 1976 confrontation the URW represented workers responsible for less than one-half of all domestic production, altogether some 6,000 fewer. Unionization of the relevant work force deteriorated as a result of erosion of established bargaining units through job-displacing mechanization in tire-making and URW inability to follow the industry into new geographic locations. Prospects for achieving "union-free" operations in the future by relocating their plants away from traditional union strongholds and offering good wages and benefits has not gone unnoticed by industry officials. "We're intelligent employers," a Goodrich executive observed on the eve of the 1979 tire contract negotiations. "We don't pay low wages, we have good benefit levels. In short, we don't do the things we did back in the 1930s that got us organized in the first place."[18]

Bituminous Coal. Bituminous, or soft, coal is an industry known for its high wages and hazardous working conditions. Both mark the historic development of labor relations in coal mining. This history includes an era of labor-capital animosity amid repeated failed attempts to stabilize product and labor markets, the post World War II years of structural consolidation of the industry and organizational cooperation between the United Mine Workers union and the operators' association that bordered on collusion, and the present period of industry instability, a return to labor strife, and declining union power.

Over the first half of this century the Mine Workers (UMW) leadership centralized authority inside the union and worked to bring about a similar consolidation of the industry. Their objective was that the head of the union might .sit down with the head of the industry and negotiate a contract binding upon every coal miner and bituminous mine operation in the country. Decades of repeating the same destructive sequence of events had convinced them that this was the most workable solution. In a period of upswing in coal, prices would rise, UMW organization would expand, and a putative national wage-and-benefit pattern would be negotiated between the UMW and the most favorably located and prosperous segments of the industry. But good times invariably gave way to bad, and the process soon was reversed. Previously closed marginal mines were reopened and production in others expanded, driving coal prices below costs of production for a substantial portion of the industry. This led to pressures on unionized operators to nullify their agreements with the UMW in order to remain price competitive with nonunion companies. When this happened, the union lost considerable membership and much of the momentum it had gathered toward organizing new fields. Through it all the UMW was without serious rivals in its organization efforts and remained ready to negotiate with the operators on a centralized basis if the latter could overcome their competitive structure.[19]

The desired consolidation occurred in 1950 with the formation of the Bituminous Coal Operators Association (BCOA). BCOA represented an alliance of large northern operators—themselves the products of an earlier merger movement in the industry—basic steel companies having extensive "captive" mine properties, and smaller operators in the south. Up to that time the union had had to negotiate separately with representatives of each of these groups, a condition creating generally unstable labor relations in the industry. A mutuality of interests between UMW and BCOA was apparent. The union wished to eliminate competition from nonunion miners, either by organizing them or by keeping their production off the major coal markets. The BCOA wanted the same noncompetitive conditions. To accomplish the common purpose, a national bituminous coal agreement was negotiated between UMW president, John L. Lewis, and northern BCOA spokesmen. Over time a Protective Wage Clause was added to (1) guarantee the organizational status of UMW as exclusive bargaining agent for the employees of all BCOA affiliates in return for a UMW commitment not to sign labor contracts with non-BCOA operators, (2) prohibit BCOA members from buying and then reselling coal mined from non-BCOA properties, (3) establish a joint union-management committee to police industry marketing practices and punish violators. Nonunion southern mines were the obvious target of the clause. So effective was the arrangement that the signatories soon found themselves side by side, shuffling back and forth between the NLRB and the federal courts to answer unfair labor charges and antitrust indictments.[20]

Part of the new labor-capital partnership in mining was UMW acceptance of job-displacing mechanization in the mines in order to give coal a price advantage over the more convenient energy substitutes. The effect on production-employment ratios was severe. In 1950 7,429 mines produced 516.3 million tons of coal with an estimated 416,000 miners, each miner averaging 6.77 tons mined per day; in 1968 5,327 mines yielded 545.3 million tons using 130,000 miners, each averaging 19.2 tons a day.[21] Wages remained high, the negotiated increases surpassing those in manufacturing generally, but fringe benefits began to lag. This was because the union failed to negotiate higher per-ton royalties with which to fund the miners' pension plan. Inadequate pension payments and arbitrary disqualifications for benefits followed. In addition the chain of miners' hospitals built and maintained throughout Appalachia out of the tonnage royalties was deteriorating.

Rapid erosion of its standards brought the union to an internal crisis. During 1969–73 the UMW was torn apart by the desperate attempts of Lewis' successor, Tony Boyle, and his supporters to retain control of the organization. They engaged in financial mismanagement, political firings of union officials, collusion with mine owners, and, finally, the hired murder of Jock Yablonsky, who had challenged Boyle in the union's presidential elections. Boyle's discredited leadership position probably contributed to the 1971 nationwide bituminous coal strike, the first since formation of the BCOA. The contract he negotiated was rejected by the rank and file because it sacrificed important local-union demands on mine health and safety issues and welfare-fund royalty payments in exchange for substantial wage increases. Despite the expected power of incumbent national union officers in these situations, a coalition of opposition elements was able to elect reform candidate Arnold Miller to the presidency and several others from his ticket to UMW executive offices and board positions. In the interim, however, the union had fallen considerably behind the rapid changes occurring in the energy industry.

The new leadership immediately was confronted with the threatening effects of structural and technological changes. These had been evident for some time but were ignored by Boyle's administration.

Two structural threats appeared.[22] First, soft-coal production was being shifted from eastern to western fields, from Appalachian and Central States deep mines to western strip mines. During 1972–76 the latter doubled their share of industry output. The different technology used in strip-mining enables operators to take out three times as much coal as in deep mines in the same number of work hours.

For the UMW this geographic movement posed a special danger. It necessitated organization efforts not only outside the union's traditional area of strength but among nonminers. Strip-mine production employees are frequently heavy-equipment operators. While the UMW has organized such workers in the east and at some western locations, other unions including the AFL-CIO Operating Engineers union—a strong and geographically centralized organization west of the Mississippi— are also active in the field and have won representation rights at strip-mine operations. This multiunion activity has fragmented coal bargaining structures. In 1977 western strip-mine negotiations led to a series of strikes and ended with separate contracts being signed on a company rather than industry basis and with the UMW controlling only 30 percent of western production. UMW was not able to organize fully the relevant work force in its industry and witnessed a crumbling of its centralized bargaining.

The second change affecting coal bargaining is growing ownership control by major oil companies of domestic coal reserves. In 1976 oil companies controlled 45 percent of these reserves (while accounting for only 21 percent of industry production). Big oil's impact on coal negotiations became apparent during the 1977–78 talks. Rank-and-file involvement in the formulation of UMW contract demands, a new experience for the industry, brought to the forefront two issues previously neglected by union negotiators: legitimizing the right of UMW locals to strike over mine-safety issues and the restoration of a national health and retirement fund. These demands were in direct opposition to the BCOA's bargaining position, which emphasize increased deep-mine productivity and curbs by the national union on local wildcat strikes. Negotiations collapsed with the sides still far apart, and a strike was called. With only 50 percent UMW control over domestic coal production, substantial stockpiles by utilities and other major coal users, and a low level of production operations in the steel industry at that time, the union was in a relatively weak bargaining position. That the strike became the longest in coal history is testimony to rank-and-file militancy and the serious nature of their demands. Apparently confident of their tactical superiority, however, BCOA negotiators rejected repeated UMW concessions and compromises and forced the union leadership to take an inferior settlement to the elected bargaining-council members for approval. They turned it down decisively.

At this stage in the deadlock a separate agreement was reached between UMW and Pittsburgh and Midway Coal (P & M), a subsidiary of Gulf Oil and a non-BCOA operator. It met most of the union's economic demands and, more important, omitted BCOA insistence on automatic penalties for wildcat strikes and its proposals on mine productivity. Neither issue held much significance for P & M, which is primarily a western strip-miner, because of the relative absence of unauthorized strikes in western mining and the high productivity levels. BCOA negotiators reportedly "fumed" at the P & M contract and stuck to their initial position, but now they offered to arbitrate their differences with the union. Armed with the P & M settlement, however, UMW bargaining-council members voted to accept nationally nothing less from the BCOA. Federal government pressure on the

BCOA to accept the P & M pattern under threat of mine seizure and operation, and a growing split inside the association between coal and steel company representatives, broke the deadlock and eventually produced a UMW-BCOA settlement close to P & M's.

By promoting the P & M contract as an industry pattern UMW leaders solved their immediate bargaining difficulty, but they hastened the movement toward a fragmented negotiating structure in future talks. The trend toward oil-based energy conglomerates, the advances being made by competitive unions in coal mining, and the expressed determination of coal-mining oil companies to resist association bargaining and even to introduce mine-by-mine incentive systems in their surface mining operations, make it unlikely that nationwide soft-coal bargaining will survive another round or two of contract negotiations.

Indeed, such a decentralized bargaining structure is almost assured by the withdrawal from the BCOA of Consolidation Coal Company, the largest employer in the association. Significantly, Consolidation is mainly a deep-mine operator. Its departure statement indicates the UMW will have to negotiate separately with it in 1981 over the same industry demands that intensified the 1978 strike. Consolidation's new president is from the firm's parent company, Continental Oil, where he negotiated labor contracts on a fragmented basis and reportedly was regarded as being a hard negotiator by the unions.[23]

Printing. Changes in industry structure and technology are eroding the bargaining power of traditionally strong craft unions in newspaper and commercial printing. This development is of more than nostalgic interest despite the relatively small-sized plants involved and the structurally deconcentrated nature of the industry. Newspaper publishing is the third-largest industry source of manufacturing employment in the nation after auto and steel.

Though historically fragmented, daily-newspaper ownership is today becoming concentrated in national chains, so much so that serious political questions are being raised about the impact on democratic decision-making processes of these holding companies. The effect on newspaper unions is more obvious and direct. Because newspapers traditionally were locally owned and controlled, printing and other craft unions organized workers and negotiated contracts at that level. Economic tests of strength to determine working conditions and terms were conducted locally. Militant unions like the Typesetters (ITU), whose members were indispensable to the production process, occupied the strongest bargaining positions and therefore set wage-and-benefit patterns for the others. Publishers in metropolitan areas usually banded together in employer associations to avoid being whipsawed by the unions; often they also arranged mutual-aid pacts to defend against selective union strikes aimed at isolating them. But chain ownership enables publishers to subsidize a struck paper in one community from the revenues of papers in other locations. As a result, individual papers in the chains have been insisting upon major concessions in contract language or economic standards, knowing that they can do without the lost revenues if the unions strike. Or they may even choose to continue publishing during a strike.

A number of such lengthy disputes have occured in recent years. Gannett Newspapers, Media General, Newhouse Newspapers, and Capital Cities Communications are some of the chains involved. They specialize in acquiring single papers in small and medium-sized communities. Among the most profitable publishers, they are known not for their journalistic excellence but rather for their ability to raise advertising revenues while cutting production costs. Capital Cities, the twelfth-largest newspaper chain in the nation and owner of more than a dozen radio and TV stations, has had lengthy labor disputes involving at least two of its papers. The most recent of these is the *Wilkes-Barre* (Pa.) *Time-Leader*, a daily acquired by Capital Cities in 1978. Within months of the acquisition local management insisted their craft unions give up previously negotiated protective working rules. The ensuing strike took on a corporatewide dimension when strikebreakers from other subsidiaries were brought into the plant to work under armed guard. A rash of violent confrontations followed between union pickets and members of the company's hired security agency. Six months after it began, the strike was still in progress.[24]

A different type of corporate reorganization is taking place among big-city and national dailies. The *New York Times, Washington Post,* and *Wall Street Journal* (Dow Jones) are examples. Large newspaper publishers are becoming diversified publishing holding companies. Their operating subsidiaries include vertically integrated acquisitions. Newsprint manufacturing properties are added to existing and acquired printing plants to make the operation more self-sufficient and immune from labor trouble. Such broad diversification also gives them formidable financial leverage in economic situations involving a single unit.

Printers, pressmen, writers, and other newspaper crafts have not been able to offset the concentrated power of these publishers. The publishers themselves are well aware of this. James Reston, columnist and now board member of the *New York Times,* observed recently that if the paper was faced with a labor problem "we would not have to take an economic strike that would in any way jeopardize the life of the paper, because the outside publications could carry it indefinitely."[25] He was referring to properties owned by the parent holding company of the *Times:* ten newspapers, three national magazines, three book publishers, two broadcasting stations, a data-storage firm, and a microfilm business. This financial capability was instrumental to the *Times* in its successful effort to persuade the historically powerful Local 6 of the ITU to accept a plan that will eventually mean the demise of the craft through gradual job attrition in the face of automated composition processes. In the same way the *Washington Post*'s integrated structure made it possible for it to continue production and circulation of the *Post* during a long strike by printing pressmen who were opposing work rule and other changes insisted upon by the publisher.[26]

Changing technology is a second and often more important source of declining union strength in the newspaper industry. In newspaper plants today a single automatic photocomposition machine can put out the same number of newspaper lines per minute that two hundred Linotype operators could in the past. With the machines having rid publishers of their need for skilled typesetters the leverage is on their side of the bargaining table. Job action by printers threatened with job displacement are merely delaying actions. Attrition agreements in which incumbent journeymen printers are assured lifetime employment—though not necessarily at their trade—are in force in some cities, but in others no such publisher commitment can be negotiated. Some craft locals, as in Kansas City, have been broken in job-related confrontations with chain publishers. The same is true in the editorial rooms, where machines also eliminate the need for human labor. The first labor-relations decision made by newspaper-chain entrepreneur Robert Murdoch upon taking ownership control of the financially ailing *New York Post* was to fire 124 editorial and advertising personnel to make way for the installation of cost-saving automated equipment.[27]

Commercial printing is also changing in ways that are damaging to printer unions. Traditional union strength depended on their ability to organize the relevant work forces in the ten largest printing centers. Together these centers contained nearly two-fifths of the nation's commercial printing establishments and accounted for one-half of the jobs and more than half the revenues. Concentration of work in these noncompeting geographic locations together with clearly defined skill demarcations on the job gave the unions sufficient bargaining strength to stabilize wages and working conditions at generally high levels.

.All this began to change during the 1960s. The conglomerate merger movement brought hundreds of previously independent commercial print shops into highly diversified corporate structures, either as in-house printing facilities or as parts of larger, horizontally integrated printing divisions. Existing printing companies sometimes extended their operations into new regions by acquiring other shops. Elsewhere companies often closed aging plants in the traditional printing centers and opened new ones in nonunion rural or southern communities. And for the first time chain-owned print shops began to appear. The overall effect was to break up the historic concentrations in commercial printing and fragment much of the industry's production outside the organizational reach of the unions. Union ability to keep the relevant work forces organized was thus lost.

Technological changes in printing machinery have in

addition destroyed craft lines, throwing the previously secure craft organizations into competition and displacing large numbers of tradesmen in some areas while creating jobs elsewhere. Photoengravers have benefited, for example, as linotype operators have become displaced. Average plant investment per production worker nearly doubled in the decade after 1961. Heavy capital expenditure requirements in turn accelerate acquisitions in printing as marginal firms find they cannot obtain necessary funds to continue on their own. This trend prompted the industry trade journal to predict "only two sizes of printing companies in about five years: the very large firm with sophisticated management and equipment, and the very small plant with a single owner and less than $250,000 in sales." Medium-sized firms are also seen to be disappearing. "The plants selling and producing $350,000 to $10 million will most likely become part of larger companies due to increased costs of doing business."[28]

Because industry consolidation and new technology most affect the traditional printing centers, it is union rather than nonunion printers who are threatened. As in the newspaper industry, commercial printing jobs are being lost and the crafts are making contract concessions. In some instances large-job print shops have been relocated outside a printing center. Management then encourages unionization of the work force by an industrial union rather than the customary crafts; a single contract calling for just one "composite" craft job is negotiated instead of several craft agreements, each with its separate craft distinction. Considerable labor-cost savings result. A few of the craft unions have responded by merging to form an industrial-type union, the Graphic Arts International Union. It now embraces most of the typical crafts found in print shops but at the same time recognizes their respective job distinctions, an approach which allows workers in the declining segments of the industry to retrain for and transfer into the expanding areas. Even so the lithographers, which is the most progressive of the crafts in printing, are barely able to keep pace with the industry.

Building Construction. Labor economists long ago recognized the potential bargaining strength of local building-trades unions. Unlike the industrial unions, they did not have to depend on national union organizing and centralized bargaining structures. This is because they typically function in "spatial monopoly" situations. Writing in 1912, an economist of the structuralist persuasion identified the sources of bargaining strength in the building-trades unions.

> The late formation of the national organizations is one reason for the decentralization which exists in the building trades, and is in turn due to the fact that the commodity produced by a workingman in the building trades cannot be transported. It is only when every unit of the commodity produced comes into competition with every other unit that the necessity for equality of wages and working conditions arises. . . . The movement of men to and from different points is a factor which tends to equalize conditions; but commodities move more freely than men, and when demands are being made the unions are better able to keep men out of the locality. It is because of these peculiarities that the building trades with weak central unions have been able to secure higher wages, shorter hours of work and improved working conditions, and throughout to attain through locals what in other trades would be done through nationals.[29]

Yet in subsequent years the centralizing tendencies of industrial prefabrication and the appearance of regional and national construction firms gave added authority to the national office in building-trades unions.[30] Labor relations nevertheless continued to be characterized by local bargaining with high wages and strong union work rules.

Current trends in technology and industrial structure are changing this. Persistent high wage increases and costly work rules, on the one hand, and skill-displacing technological changes and an availability of workers having enough skill to do the work, on the other, have encouraged the rise of employer associations intent on operating union-free. Their success in this is an accurate measure of the extent to which the unions in some construction labor markets have allowed the relevant work force to be moved beyond the scope of their contracts.

Associated Builders and Contractors (ABC), the largest of the nonunion employers association, started to grow nationally in the late 1960s and by 1972 claimed some four thousand members. The union-free issue was joined that year when direct confrontations occurred between Philadelphia area trades and an outspoken, aggressive ABC firm, Altemose Construction Co. Altemose claimed to be a "merit shop" instead of either a union or open (no-union) shop operation, and that both union and nonunion workers were employed. In practice, no union tradesmen stayed on Altemose projects. Union representatives acknowledged an average $1.50-per-hour wage differential between "merit" and union contractors.[31] But the trades were not able to stop Altemose and other ABC firms from completing projects.

Reliable figures are not available, but earlier estimations of ABC strength by union contractors, who might have been inclined to exaggerate the threat in order to impress upon unions the need to moderate their money demands, were that in 1971 the nonunion contractors accounted for one-third of all industrial construction nationally. Industrial jobs are the strongholds of building-trades power, residential construction never having been strongly unionized.[32] Today ABC says more than half the nation's commercial building is done by nonunion labor. Member contractors claim even greater proportions; California's 1200 affiliates insist they have a dominant share of the work in many parts of the state.[33]

The relative isolation of individual labor markets, an important source of the "spatial-monopoly" element in traditional construction-union bargaining power, is disappearing due to the rise of nationwide contractors. Such employers can bid on major construction projects anywhere in the country because they are large, mobile firms with both the expertise and capital equipment to be competitive. In addition, advances in various forms of prefabricated building material, such as precast concrete, undermine the craft basis of union-bargaining leverage by eliminating or reducing the employer's need for certain job skills.

To meet these threats, local and area building-trades unions have made concessions. Unable to influence decisions and practices at the earlier stages of the construction business, they have to confront the problem at the job site, where they must sacrifice job standards to the point that union labor costs little more than the alternative labor source, construction technique, or contracting firms. Faced with four of every five of their members out of work, a New York City bricklayers local union accepted a wage-and-benefit reduction negotiated by their international union to discourage substitution of nonunion labor and prefabricated materials for union labor and hand-built masonry.[34]

The Washington, D.C., building-trades council agreed to long-term concessions in their affiliated-members' contracts in order to help make area contractors cost-competitive with nonunion firms. Among other things they took a no-strike pledge and reduced workmen's compensation insurance benefits; the locals indicated they may retain existing compensation benefits by paying the differences in premium costs from their dues monies. Acknowledging the nationwide trend in agreements of this kind, an official of the AFL-CIO Building Trades Department commented: "This is one way to strengthen the construction trades—to offer employers eight hours work for eight hours pay."[35]

Construction unions have not, however, found a way to cope with "double-breasting," an additional threat to their established bargaining positions. A "double-breasted" structure exists where the same firm owns union and nonunion construction companies, presumably using the unionized subsidiary for projects requiring union labor and the nonunion division in competitive-bid situations involving both union and nonunion firms. Double-breasting is not illegal. The National Labor Relations Board has ruled that commonly owned but separately operated companies are separate employers for labor-relations purposes.[36] Building-trades officials nevertheless fear a gradual diversion of work within double-breasted firms from the union to the nonunion division. Fragmentary evidence supports their concern. For example, Peter Kiewit, a union firm, collapsed its regular Oklahoma operations after establishing a nonunion shop. That contractors see the value of double-breasted structures is evident from the growing competi-

tion among union contractors to acquire nonunion subsidiaries. Fluor, a union firm and the nation's second
largest contractor, recently bought Daniel International,
nonunion and the eleventh largest.[37]

Chemical and Steel. Two additional basic industries show a
current weakening of union organizational strength.
Some chemical and steelmaking firms have aggressively
either displaced incumbent local unions or kept out
petitioning unions from their multiunit operation. It is
essential for unions in these horizontally consolidated,
national-product industries to organize and bring under
common terms and conditions of employment all the
domestic production workers of each firm. Production
that occurs outside the scope of union organization
threatens established contract standards.

Dow Chemical Company, the nation's largest chemical
producer, has undertaken a remarkably successful antiunion effort. In 1969 22 of Dow's plants were unionized; in 1976 just 7 plants remained organized. Workers
in 15 of them decertified their unions in labor board
elections.[38] This number of decertifications is unprece-
dented. Why would workers reject their union like this?
At least three reasons appear. First, chemical companies
pay above-average wages and have the ability to pay
higher wages if necessary. Unions are not necessary to
the workers for satisfactory earnings and benefits—at
least in the short run. Second, several unions have representation rights in Dow plants, and their bargaining
structures are fragmented on a plant-by-plant basis, with
no single plant accounting for a significant share of total
production. This segmentation makes the unions vulnerable to whipsawing tactics by Dow. Third, though it is
illegal for employers to involve themselves directly in
employee self-determination elections, the law is ineffec-

tual against an employer who is determined to operate union-free.

Dow used two strategies in its decertification program. One is to convert hourly workers to salaried employees. This new employment status substitutes the individual rewards and privileges associated with white-collar employment for the negotiated standards under collective bargaining. Upon the decertification of an incumbent union immediate economic improvements are put in effect. The second strategy involves individual "job enrichment," in which the worker has greater discretion over his or her performance of direct job tasks. One Dow executive explained the underlying philosophy at a company conference for managers.

> I think the greatest advantage afforded us by a salaried operation is that our people can be motivated to strive for maximum achievement when they learn that they can be identified and rewarded for superior achievement and accomplishment.

> Under any system people with closely defined and repetitive tasks, in structured, fractionated jobs are driven toward alternate organizations, including unions, to relieve frustration and boredom.[39]

Circumventing legally certified unions in order to replace them with direct employer-employee relationships frequently involves Dow in unfair labor-practice convictions.[40] Yet neither National Labor Relations Board nor federal court remedies have dissuaded Dow from pursuing its policy. Nor have the unions been able to deter the company through job actions. They cannot strike effectively against Dow because the plants are operationally segmented. Production in one unit normally is independent of that in others. And, moreover, chemical production processes are such that the large number of salaried (nonunion) personnel can operate the plants for long periods of time in the absence of the regular production and maintenance work force.[41] Thus, the more extensive is Dow's policy of converting production jobs to salaried functions, the more effective its decertification program becomes.

Basic steel presents a quite different union problem. Long ago the Steelworkers union organized the major producers. It then followed them wherever they went within the United States to produce steel. Now, however, emerging southern steel firms are frustrating steel unionization. In addition, if a particular mill does become organized, they simply refuse to recognize and bargain with the union. Their resistance often entails labor-law violations by them, but judicial remedies have had no apparent impact on the success of their resistance. Florida Steel, the nation's twenty-fifth-ranked steel company, but one of the fastest growing, makes and fabricates steel in 17 mills located in three southeastern states. It produces primarily for the southern market and is one of the few domestic steel companies that is currently increasing significantly its total steelmaking capacity.[42]

In 1973 the United Steelworkers, recognizing the potential danger posed by these nonunion facilities to its national contracts, initiated a major organizing drive against Florida Steel. Its strategy called for unionization of the company's three steel-producing facilities, each of which uses the most advanced furnace and rolling-mill technology available, and then move into its fabricating plants. Three years later the drive had failed, but Florida Steel either had been found guilty of violating the national labor law or had agreed to make back-pay settlements to workers fired for union activity in 15 separate labor board cases; in five the company was cited for contempt by federal appeal courts for refusing to obey prior board orders in connection with its illegal acts. Fourteen additional union charges were pending.

Despite these illegal acts by Florida Steel, the union won worker elections in two of the three steel mills. Yet after nearly two years of bargaining, the union was unable to negotiate a contract at either location. This failure in turn contributed to its election defeat at the third mill. During negotiations Florida Steel refused to increase wages and benefits at the unionized mills by the same amount as its unilateral increases in the nonunion mills until ordered to do so by the labor board.[43] In its order the board concluded Florida Steel's "history of unfair labor practices" and "other types of flagrant violations" reveal "a course of unlawful conduct taken . . . in the service of designs inimical to the collective bargaining process." It noted that two-and-one-half years after the union won the election in a North Carolina mill "there is no evidence that any meaningful collective bargaining has taken place."[44]

Eventually the United Steelworkers may organize Florida Steel and other nonunion southern steel firms.[45] It may even bring them under the terms of the basic steel agreement. But the resistance of these expanding firms against a formidable labor organization dramatizes the change that has occurred in the labor movement's relative power position since the 1930s.

This union also faces new corporate opposition in medium-sized northern firms. Many of these have been acquired by diversified corporations which then try to weaken established industry patterns in their subsidiaries. An example is Timkin Roller Bearing's take-over of Latrobe Steel, a high alloy steelmaker. Shortly after the acquisition Latrobe and the steelworkers union began negotiating the 1977 contract. It had been customary for the parties to settle within the industry pattern. But this time Latrobe agreed to meet the economic settlement reached earlier in Big Steel negotiations, while it insisted on contract language changes in nearly two-dozen sections of the agreement, many of which covered traditional working standards. In addition, Latrobe wanted to change the expiration date of the contract from the rest of the industry; a different expiration date would break away Latrobe's negotiations from future steel bargaining.

The local struck in August 1977. In February 1978, with neither side having modified its position, striking workers voted almost unanimously to continue the walkout. The international union characterized Timkin's bargaining objective as "a testing of the 'me-too' pattern concept of expanding the basic steel agreement to hundreds of smaller steel companies and producers."[46] The following month Latrobe management warned strikers that "it would be fruitless to attempt to do business in the competitive environment of today" unless the plant's work rules were modified to enable the company to offset the costly economic package in basic steel. Unless Latrobe's final offer, which had not changed essentially since February, was accepted by the workers, they said, "there will be no jobs at Latrobe Steel."[47] Aware that other Timkin plants had been closed during strikes, the workers voted to go back exactly nine months after having struck. The union conceded in half the disputed contract provisions.[48]

Manufacturing Supply and Fabricating

The capital mobility associated with conglomerate and multinational corporate structures, together with the law's inability to discourage employer repeat violations in some instances, have reversed union gains in widening negotiated wage-and-benefit standards in primary manufacturing industries to include supply and fabricating sectors. This has been the case in roller-bearing and steel-fabricating industries and in other industries including motor-vehicle wheels, rubber footwear, and paper products. Small- or medium-sized firms typically are acquired by diversified companies that have alternative production capabilities. Under the consolidated ownership, subsidiary management demands union contract concessions by using the threat of plant closure or partial shutdown. This sometimes occurs either at the outset or after a lengthy strike. In any event, even after union concessions the plant may be kept open only a few years longer.

Brass products. Several conglomerate employers have either closed the plants of their acquired brass-products subsidiaries or have negotiated substantial union concessions. Operations were sometimes resumed in southern locations, where they remain unorganized. Affected plants include the brass divisions of National Distillers, Scoville Manufacturing, Kennecott, Anaconda (an integrated nonferrous metals company now owned by the ARCO energy conglomerate), and U-V industries.

Scoville is a traditional brass fabricator that diversified by acquiring firms in unrelated product lines such as metal fasteners and by selling its Connecticut "Brass Valley" plants. Before divesting the brass division in 1976, Scoville threatened to close the plant unless the UAW local there agreed to rescind scheduled wage increases and fringe-benefit improvements. Some 1800 hourly workers were affected. Union acceptance, it was later learned, had been a condition of Century Brass Products' purchase of Scoville's brass operations. Also in

Connecticut, workers at Bridgeport Brass took economic cuts and agreed to a three-year moratorium on fringe benefits in return for a commitment from the parent company, National Distillers, that it would continue limited operations. This followed a 42 percent reduction in the plant's work force and a threat to close the facility entirely.[49]

U-V Industries phased down much of its Mueller Brass operations in Michigan and expanded those in Mississippi. This firm is vertically integrated. Among other things it mines and smelts nonferrous metal ores, fabricates copper and brass products, and uses them in the manufacture of electrical components for the building and construction industry. A pattern of plant relocation from union to nonunion regions and of unfair labor practices in the course of resisting unionization efforts is found throughout the company integrated structure.

During a 1972 Auto Workers union strike at U-V's Michigan subsidiary, the company announced a partial shutdown. The announcement deflated union demands and ended the strike. But organized labor was not able to follow the work. Since 1971 the Steelworkers union has tried without success to organize the Mississippi plant. Mueller Brass, the subsidiary, three times has been found guilty of illegally interfering with the union's efforts by intimidating and firing or otherwise discriminating against employees sympathetic to the union.[50]

During this time U-V's major electrical-components manufacturing subsidiary, Federal Pacific Corporation, acquired in 1970, began phasing out production in its northern plants and expanding operations at a new facility in North Carolina. The electrical workers union (IBEW) succeeded in organizing the southern plant in 1971, but Federal Pacific refused to bargain with the union. Instead, according to the National Labor Relations Board, it was illegally "soliciting an employee to circulate a decertification petition" and "threatening an employee that it would leave North Carolina and go back north before it would sign a contract."[51] Continued refusal to bargain resulted in a direct board order—an infrequent measure—to bargain with the IBEW.[52] Finally, unable to win a contract, the IBEW struck the North Carolina plant. After a protracted walkout the parties signed an agreement, not because the union had overwhelming power in the plant, but because Federal Pacific was vulnerable to the nationwide boycott of its building and construction materials by members of other building-trades unions, a weakness not generally shared by southern manufacturing subsidiaries.

A final instance of deteriorating union power in brass fabricating involves a six-month strike during 1977–78 by the steelworkers union and two others against six plants of ASARCO. In the end the unions had to make concessions in contract language concerning job security and working conditions.

Poor union settlements in the leading sectors of an industry set the pattern for negotiations elsewhere. During the final month of the ASARCO strike and after other unions had made concessions in brass fabricating, management negotiators at a Pennsylvania plant of Cerro Brass demanded economic relief. Cerro is owned by a family-controlled holding company, which means the union does not know the financial condition of the parent company or its individual subsidiaries because it is not a public corporation. Unless the union agreed to cost-cutting measures, Cerro negotiators claimed, future plant operations would be in jeopardy. Three years earlier, the union, a UAW local, had struck for 39 days over economic issues. This time the members accepted, though by a modest majority, a 25-cents-per-hour wage package over three years in return for additional economic security benefits in the event of a plant closure.[53]

Roller Bearings. The domestic roller-bearing industry has shut down plants and relocated production to nonunion areas in response to price competitive imports. Unions have had differential success following work.

Dominated by a few producers, the domestic bearing industry has been quite profitable, inviting foreign penetration of its market. Japanese bearing producers alone increased their sales in this country nearly twelve-fold in the decade following 1962; bearing prices fell by one-fifth. Higher U.S. tariffs in 1974 stanched the flow somewhat, but by then the two major domestic bearing producers were already migrating south.[54]

Between 1970–75 Federal Mogul opened six plants in the south, while it was closing four Michigan plants and a warehouse and distribution center; it also has sixteen overseas bearing operations. Timkin, also a substantial overseas producer, moved some of its northern production to a South Carolina plant. Hoover Ball and Bearing, by contrast, divested its domestic bearing operations to a Japanese firm and conglomerated itself into other product lines.

Federal Mogul and Timkin committed labor-law violations in trying to maintain union-free production in their southern plants.[55] Despite Federal Mogul's unfair labor practices at its Alabama plant the United Auto Workers won recognition rights in 1976 after a third election attempt.

Foreign-owned multinational corporations pose similar threats to established domestic unions in supply and fabricating industries. In addition, the threat is more complicated because final decision-making is by overseas executives who are of course unaccountable to U.S. labor representatives.

The phasing down of Copperweld Corporation's main production plant in Pennsylvania exemplifies the problem. In 1975 Copperweld, a bimetallic fabricator, was acquired by Société Imetal (SI), an integrated French-based mining-and-metal-manufacturing combine. SI is controlled by the Rothschild family holding company, but a minority interest is owned by Amax, the U.S. mining conglomerate. Acquisition of Copperweld made SI one of the largest foreign investors in the U.S. and gave it control of the country's principal copper-coated wire producer. Previously Copperweld had developed an improved production technique that results in higher quality bimetallics using fewer hourly workers. This technological edge plus Copperweld's superior profit performance in recent years made it an attractive takeover target. Both Copperweld management and the Steelworkers union, which represents workers at the Glassport plant, initially resisted SI's efforts. They initiated special legislative action to block the acquisition. During Congressional hearings on the proposed takeover SI owners gave official assurances they would not dismantle existing Copperweld operations. "I cannot emphasize strongly enough that we do not intend to withdraw jobs, plants, know-how or elements of Copperweld's business," Baron Guy de Rothschild promised in a statement submitted to the House investigating subcommittee.[56] After a federal judge refused to enjoin the acquisition, Copperweld managers abandoned their effort and the combination was completed.

Negotiations between Copperweld's Pennsylvania plant management and the union reached an impasse in the first round of contract bargaining following the acquisition. Copperweld demanded local union concessions in contract language regarding work rules and crew sizes. The union extended the contract rather than strike, however. This was Copperweld's oldest bimetallic plant, and the new technology was scheduled to be installed at a newer, nonunion Copperweld plant in Tennessee. Alternative production capacity made a strike ineffective. The Pennsylvania local in fact had struck for seven weeks in 1967 in an unsuccessful multilocal attempt to establish common contract expiration dates at three Copperweld plants where the Steelworkers held bargaining rights. Their objective had been to bring greater economic leverage against Copperweld in future negotiations by being able to threaten simultaneous closure of all three plants.

This time production continued three months at the Pennsylvania facility without a new contract being signed. Copperweld then announced plans to close its operation there, citing declining product sales, outmoded plant and equipment, and failure to renegotiate the contract. After some delay a final decision was made by the company to stop all copper-coating work but to continue and retain the aluminum processing there; this would eliminate two-thirds of roughly 600 production jobs in the plant. The union then agreed to most of the company's proposed contract changes in order to keep the aluminum work in Pennsylvania.[57]

Despite the occasional foray into industrial conflict by domestic subsidiaries of foreign multinationals, the U.S.-based conglomerate corporation is still the *bête noire* of production workers in the industrial areas of the northeast and midwest. Litton Industries is a leading example. Litton acquired and subsequently shut down numerous manufacturing plants, including those in the electric-calculator, shipbuilding, typewriter, electric-motor, and rubber-products industries. Its subsidiary managers have imposed concession bargaining on local unions in these and other situations.[58]

Examination of labor relations in Litton's domestic subsidiaries reveals a pattern of systematic and aggressive antiunion behavior. Overall, the company has successfully kept nonunion operations unorganized and weakened or ousted incumbent unions in its acquired properties. Union organizing drives routinely are met with job threats, intimidation, and discipline of union sympathizers, as well as unilateral improvements in wages, benefits, and working conditions. Newly certified unions are sometimes simply not recognized for bargaining purposes by Litton subsidiaries despite their legal standing, or they are unable to negotiate a first contract. Time delays of one and two years between the time workers vote in favor of union representation and commencement of negotiations are common. Established unions are undermined through company initiated or assisted efforts at decertifying them, bargaining threats to close plants, and ultimatum bargaining, in which subsidiary demands for union concessions are made on a take-it-or-leave-it basis.

These practices frequently result in labor-law violations. Between 1963 and 1975 some 22 Litton subsidiary operations were named in 29 separate complaints issued by counsel for the NLRB. A variety of unfair labor practices were alleged. Consent agreements between the company and the government or the union involved settled many of them prior to board hearings. Of the 18 cases that eventually had to be decided by the board, Litton subsidiaries were found in violation of the law in 13, in a total of 18 counts. These include eight illegal interferences in worker elections, four instances of illegal refusal to bargain, three illegal implementations of wage-and-benefit improvements during union-organizing drives, two illegal establishments of company-dominated worker organizations, and one illegal firing of a union member.[59]

Yet it is inconceivable that the kind of board and federal court remedies so far imposed against Litton and its subsidiaries would dissuade the company from its demonstrated labor policy. The National Labor Relations Act is remedial rather than punitive in intent. In practice this means the object of administrative and court proceedings is not to punish offenders but to restore a previolation environment from which stable labor relations can be resumed. Specific remedies are normally limited to reinstatement with back pay for employees discriminated against for their union activities and the posting of notices saying that the employer (or union) has committed unfair labor practices and will not do so again. Repeated violations simply mean more fines and posted notices. There is here an implicit presumption of compliance behavior and good faith intent by the parties. A repeat violator like Litton Industries is, with only a few exceptions, treated no differently than a first offender. It is understandable that in these circumstances an employer who chooses to violate labor law on a calculated cost-benefit basis would eventually build a remarkable record of corporate recidivism. The benefit is considerable while the cost is negligible.

One instance involving Litton Industries illustrates the point. In 1969 Litton closed the Missouri manufacturing plant of its Royal Typewriter division. It did so during a labor strike there which was later judged to have been instigated by Litton's illegal efforts to break the union and to intimidate the workers with threats to remove production facilities to Litton's other typewriter plants if they struck over new contract demands. The union brought charges, seeking reinstatement of production at the plant and full payment of certain contractual benefits owed the workers.

Final board disposition of the complaint was not made until 1974, the five-year delay being due mainly to procedural and appeal options exercised by the company. In addition, Litton's structural and managerial complexity made for protracted proceedings. It took several days of trial testimony, for example, just to unravel the maze of corporate organizations within which Litton produced and sold typewriters. In its decision the NLRB found that Litton and Royal constituted a single employer under the law, which made the parent company liable. Litton-Royal had to post notices in the now-vacant plant stating their intent to bargain with the union over undistributed pension, vacation, and other money benefits and over transfer rights of the workers to other Litton subsidiaries. Yet by 1976 no negotiations had taken place—seven years after Litton had illegally closed the plant. Litton Industries refused to deal with the union until the board's inclusion of it in the judgment was settled in appeals court; Royal refused to bargain on grounds that it cannot legally negotiate with a union over matters that involve other Litton subsidiaries in the same community where its plant had been because they are nonunion and operate under independent management.[60]

The Decline of Union Bargaining Power

Union bargaining power in the industries selected for discussion here is declining. It is not doing so in all or even most industries. But these setbacks may portend a general weakening of the labor movement. Unions in the high-wage, relatively stable industries continue to negotiate national contracts boasting general contract settlements with substantial hourly earnings and benefits, but they do so in the context of diminishing production-job opportunities. Present are the first signs of future labor-capital struggles over relative shares in a period of deteriorating performance. Foreign competition, nonunion southern production, and stagnating sales markets are beginning to erode the traditional ability of oligopolistic employers in the basic industries to pay higher labor costs and still maintain their anticipated profit margins. These changes also challenge the ability of the union to make them pay because of the expansion of the relevant work force to include inhospitable groups and regions.

Perhaps more indicative of the future are the industries in transition described above. Most of them were previously among the stable, high-earnings sectors. But changes in corporate structures and technology have disrupted union ability to organize and bring into effective bargaining structures the relevant work force.

If this transition simply reflects the ebb and flow of strength among different unions, with some increasing and others decreasing in power, then we would expect to find random movement in both directions. But we do not. The observable shifts are in the direction of declining union bargaining strength. There are perhaps some exceptions, such as unions in the cigarette and retail industries, but they do not offset the trend that is observed in the current labor-management scene.

The political economy of the situation seems reasonably clear. In our highly institutionalized, legalistic labor relations system, in which collective bargaining is the preferred public policy method of resolving industrial conflict, formal bargaining structures and organizational rights are crucial in determining relative labor-capital power. Labor's economic power rests on its ability to unionize specific groups of workers along occupational and product lines. Both trade union requirements and administrative law require unions to keep their jurisdictional lines in order and to construct bargaining units that maximize their strike effectiveness. Success in this regard hinges on specific legal interpretations and organizational judgments that are appropriate to the economic environment in a particular time period.

In the 1930s both AFL and CIO unions fashioned their respective organizational and bargaining structures to match existing industrial organization, market behavior, and production methods. Public policy was fluid. Not only did it sustain labor's organizing momentum from one industry to another through sympathetic NLRB rulings in representation matters, but it helped the new unions in mass-production and service industries to shape the formal bargaining structures to their tactical advantage. Companywide and industrywide bargaining units that embraced entire hourly work forces were found appropriate for these industries in administrative law proceedings. This gave the unions organizational control over the relevant work forces and centralized bargaining structures, conditions that were the institutional bases of their subsequent bargaining power. Unfortunately for labor, however, these favorable structures became frozen in time. Labor's own organizational rigidities and an inflexibility in administrative law in the handling of bargaining structure disputes are preserving structural arrangements rooted in the past.[61] Because the bargaining system is one in which management initiates and the union responds, labor is most disadvantaged by bargaining structures that do not conform to the current environment. Almost by definition union strength fades with time and change. We have had four decades of change since big labor's salad days.

Clearly, the dismal forecasts Lindblom and Simons

made under the spell of rampant CIO power during the 1940s have failed to materialize. Only avid antiunionists pretend that forty years of collective bargaining have altered the distribution of income in our society or jeopardized capital's dominance. Many unions do have the ability to negotiate economic terms that maintain or slightly improve their members' income share and enhance the real value of their fringe benefits. But many others do not. Nothing approaching the strike power imagined by Lindblom and Simon has existed in the American labor movement. Heads of unions which may be able to paralyze the economy, like the leadership of the International Brotherhood of Teamsters, have devoted more time and effort to finding ways of avoiding national strike actions and quelling unauthorized rank-and-file walkouts than they have given to plotting the economic ruin of the Republic. Lindblom himself now deprecates the politico-economic importance of the unions. Their relative unimportance today, he says, is explained by a global environment in which "the rules of market-oriented systems, while granting a privileged position to business, so far appear to prohibit the organizational moves that would win a comparable position for labor. Hence a privileged position for union leaders and their unions is approximated only in special circumstances."[62]

It is ironic, though, that the unions currently demonstrating the greatest bargaining effectiveness are also the most dependent on the continued well-being of their industries. This interdependency requires mutual efforts at economic protection. Witness the growing alliance between the United Steelworkers and Big Steel on the question of steel imports and, in specific instances, on the matter of environmental pollution standards. The rank-and-file millworkers sees himself with the choice of

working either for an inefficient, stagnating, environmental polluting industry or for none at all. Under the
circumstance he understandably insists his union support protectionist efforts.

Still, a number of unions find themselves beset by
changes against which they have little protection and by
an employer offensive against which they have no
adequtae defense. There is no comfort for them, however, in conventional economic analysis. To the neoclassical economic mind what is now happening to organized
labor is what should be happening. Unions priced themselves out of labor markets, and their members are now
experiencing the results. Previous union successes dis-
torted free, competitive markets and gave rise to in-
efficiencies and misallocations of labor factors. Reduced
union power, in this view, will lower production costs
and, consequently, reduce product prices at higher levels
of employment.

The problem with this analysis is that it implies labor
markets are monopolized by unions but markets are
competitive. If this were true, then organized labor indeed would present the only institutional obstruction to
an otherwise free-enterprise market system, and any
overall decline in its bargaining power would theoretically benefit everyone but the monopoly labor interests.
But this is an invalid, if heroic, assumption. Product
markets are not price competitive in concentrated or
otherwise protected industries. Unions and collective
bargaining are simply one of several institutional devices
to insulate the participants against the discipline of the
marketplace. To single out labor as being worthy of a
decline in its power is to ignore by omission the remain-
ing sources of market control and to subject labor to the
unrestrained coercion of employers. Aside from the
faithful, no one can say with confidence that destruction

of union bargaining power will result in lower product prices.

Consider the roller-bearing industry. It is busily relocating production to lower-wage regions, but we have no assurance that lower labor costs will result in lower bearing prices. Indeed, the history of this industry makes it unlikely. Federal Mogul closed northern plants and expanded southern ones, presumably realizing labor cost savings in the process. These moves enabled the company to overcome what it identified as a major obstacle to efficient production. At a 1972 conference of domestic bearing manufacturers Federal Mogul Corporation's marketing manager proposed several industry responses to foreign competition, one of which was aimed at reducing labor costs: "anti-trust action is needed where we must break up a monopoly—and that monopoly is organized labor."[63] But a Federal Trade Commission complaint issued three years later revealed that in 1972 Federal Mogul had itself violated the anti-trust laws when it entered into a secret agreement with SKF, the U.S. subsidiary of ABSKF, a Swedish bearing manufacturer and the world's largest producer. Under the agreement the two companies divided portions of the domestic bearing market. Federal Mogul stopped making small-sized bearings, leaving that market to SKF, and the latter got out of the automotive bearing market, agreeing to produce those bearings for Federal Mogul, which would then sell them to SKF's former customers.[64]

Nor is there any assurance that buyers will enjoy price reductions in commercial construction as a result of diminished union strength in that industry. Antitrust investigators recently disclosed an acknowledged 30-year history of price-fixing and project allocation among nationwide contractors like Brown & Root and J. Ray McDermott & Co. The same objection can be raised in the steel industry, where nine companies and their executives were being fined at about the same time for conspiring to fix prices of reinforced steel bars.[65] An inexhaustible list of such offenses could follow.

The question remains Why has labor not responded effectively? At least part of the explanation is its historic failure to reconcile the need to centralize bargaining structures with the need to build grass-roots understanding of threatening situations and support for appropriate union responses. Concentrated negotiating structures and internal union administration may be necessary for tactical bargaining purposes, but they also separate leaders from members, create distinctions between organizational and membership objectives in collective bargaining, promote manipulation and distrust, and transform the union into a service organization.[66] A tendency may develop for union leaders to view the rank and file as being irrational and uninformed but at the same time be wary of educating them. Should changes in the bargaining environment undermine the union's tactical position, the workers may be instinctively aware of the threat but uninformed as to its precise nature and what are the union's alternative strategies.

Labor's likely response to increasingly hostile environments requires even greater centralization, however. One alternative is to modify national labor laws to discourage repeat violators while strengthening labor's organizing efforts. Though this approach is one that nearly every segment of the labor movement can support, and did so during Congressional consideration of a reform bill in 1978, the legislation failed to get out of committee intact and was dropped, at least for the time being.

A second alternative is to consolidate unions through merger and combination and to coordinate bargaining activities among two or more unions. This solution appeals to many but not all unionists; a number of such mergers have taken place in recent years and more are underway, but prospects are dim that a handful of unions having broad product and service jurisdictions will replace the more than one hundred separate international unions existing today.

Considerable progress has been made in the coordinated bargaining area. Multiunion committees exist for more than sixty multiindustry employers. A survey of their experiences shows, however, that coordinated bargaining is most successful in multiplant, single product-line situations, such as General Electric, and least successful in highly diversified situations.[67] It does not appear to be a solution to labor's bargaining difficulties with conglomerate corporations.

The third response has the least amount of support within the labor movement. This alternative is for labor to acquire independent political power and use it in order to resolve economic problems by imposing legislative restrictions and obligations on capital. The Scandinavian labor movement is the model for this response. But making political action a priority is contrary to the dominant business-union philosophy of American unions. It has never been popular with AFL craft organizations, and in the CIO unions it is associated with the left-wing activism which divided the industrial union movement during the early Cold War period. Though independent labor political action has few open admirers inside the official house of labor, leaders of the Auto Workers, Machinists, and a handful of other unions recently established an interunion coalition pledged to support a democratic socialist legislative program. This approach means, of course, that labor will have to sympathize with and address the causes of interest to the groups it would have to join with in building a majority political coalition.

The political solution may be the only practical alternative for American labor. The traditional sources of union bargaining power relate to economic market considerations. But such power is necessarily transient because market conditions are always changing and labor has little control over such changes.

Capital ultimately controls markets because property rights bestow unilateral authority in the structural and technical conditions that dominate market relationships. For workers in industries where union strength is being undermined there is little likelihood that it will be restored through market tactics. Apparently nothing short of political power will remedy their situation.

Perhaps, however, the most likely response from the mainstream of the labor movement will be simply to do nothing. This is predictable to the extent labor history is a guide to the future. In the past, and particularly in response to a similar decline during the 1920s, organized labor chose to do nothing in the face of shrinking membership rolls and eroding bargaining power. Instead, the labor movement, meaning the craft unions and the AFL, gathered around those organizations which managed to hold members and show continued bargaining power as a result of the tactical position of certain skilled trades. But in doing so, labor ignored the bulk of the nation's workers and workplaces and became a narrow, insular institution, unable to shape industrial events and unprepared for the coming economic crisis. A similar response today would result in a contraction of labors organizational base to include those skilled trades as yet unaffected by technological changes, those industrial workers not yet displaced by structural and market changes in basic manufacturing, and those public employees who keep their jobs despite growing taxpayer attacks upon government budgets. Under these conditions organized labor would be little more than a spokesman for the special interests of the aristocrats of the working class.

NOTES

1. Henry C. Simons, "Some Reflections on Syndicalism," *Journal of Political Economy* (March 1944).

2. Charles E. Lindblom, *Unions and Capitalism* (New Haven: Yale University Press, 1949).

3. Walter P. Reuther, *Price Policy and Public Responsibility: Administered Prices in the Automobile Industry* (Detroit: UAW Publications Department, 1958), pp. 50–52. Statement presented to the Subcommittee on Anti-trust and Monopoly of the Committee on the Judiciary, U.S. Senate, January 28, 1958.

4. These structural and behavioral conditions include either horizontal or vertical consolidation or both, pricing and marketing leadership by a dominant firm or firms, "full-cost" or other formula pricing to obtain predetermined "target" rates of return on investment, and "standard volume" production levels at which unit profit margins ensure the desired rate of return. John Blair, *Economic Concentration: Structure, Behavior and Public Policy* (New York: Harcourt Brace Jovanovich, 1972), pp. 467–75.

5. E.g., see generally, Harold Levinson, Charles Rehmus, Joseph Goldberg, and Mark Kahn, eds., *Collective Bargaining and Technological Change in American Transportation* (Evanston: Transportation Center at Northwestern University, 1971). Specifically, see James Annable, Jr., "The ICC, the IBT, and the Cartelization of the American Trucking Industry," *The Quarterly Review of Economics and Business* (summer 1973): 33–48.

6. Harold Levinson, "Unionism, Concentration, and Wage Changes: Toward a Unified Theory," *Industrial and Labor Relations Review* (January 1967): 198–205.

7. Average hourly earnings in individual unionized GE assembly plants deviated by up to one-fourth from the corporation's national average, an intolerable condition for unions in a national product industry. *UE News,* November 17, 1969. From near parity following World War II, wages and benefits of electrical-product workers had fallen $2–3 per hour behind those for auto workers by 1966. David

Lasser, "A Victory for Coordinated Bargaining," *American Federationist* (April 1967). For a discussion of GE's labor policy during this period see James Healy, ed., *Creative Collective Bargaining* (Englewood Cliffs, N.J.: Prentice-Hall, 1965), pp. 52–60.

8. Charles Craypo, "Bargaining Units and Corporate Merger: NLRB Policy in the Intercity Bus Industry," *Industrial Relations Law Journal* (summer 1976): 285–322.

9. See Charles Neill, *Report on Conditions of Employment in the Iron and Steel Industry*, U.S. Senate Document No. 110, 62nd Cong., 1st Sess. (Washington, D.C.: GPO, 1913), pp. 115–23, 497–500; David Brody, *Steelworkers in America: The Nonunion Era* (New York: Harper & Row, 1960), pp. 61–68.

10. For testimony and documentation on this and similar cases, see U.S. Congress, House, *Oversight Hearings on the National Labor Relations Act*, Hearings before the Subcommittee on Labor-Management Relations of the Committee on Education and Labor, 94th Cong., 2nd Sess. (Washington, D.C.: GPO, 1976).

11. Bureau of Labor Statistics, "Collective Bargaining in the Meat Products Industry," Robert 467, 1976.

12. Jonathan Kwitney, "Embattled Butchers," *Wall Street Journal,* November 1, 1977, p. 1.

13. *Butcher Workman,* April 1977, p. 20.

14. *In These Times,* June 20–26, 1979, p. 6.

15. See *John Herling's Labor Letter,* April 28, 1973, for a discussion of how URW further fell behind the UAW in wage standards during the 1973 round of bargaining; by 1976 URW officials acknowledged a $1.65 hourly wage differential between auto and tire production workers, *Wall Street Journal,* April 16, 1976, p. 2.

16. Blair, *Economic Concentration*, pp. 31–32, 357.

17. *Wall Street Journal,* April 22, 1976, p. 2.

18. *Wall Street Journal,* February 14, 1979, p. 6.

19. Morton Baratz, *The Union and the Coal Industry* (New Haven: Yale University Press, 1955); McAllister Coleman, *Men and Coal* (New York: Farrar and Rinehart, 1943).

20. T. N. Bethell, "Conspiracy in Coal," *Washington Monthly* (March 1969).

21. *Minerals Yearbook* (1974).

22. John Schnell, "The Impact on Collective Bargaining of Oil Company Ownership of Bituminous Coal Properties," *Labor Studies Journal* (winter 1979). Discussion of the 1977–78 coal strike and settlement is based on Schnell's work.

23. Ben A. Franklin, "Future Coal Talks Clouded by Pullout," *New York Times,* May 27, 1979.

24. Irwin Aronson, "Union-Busting in Northeast Pennsylvania," *Pennsylvania AFL-CIO News,* October 1978, pp. 4–50. See also *Oakland*

Press Co. (subsidiary of Capital Cities Communications, Inc.), 29 NLRB No. 77 (1977).

25. *Washington Post,* July 25, 1977, p. D-10.

26. For an informed analysis of these and other big-city newspaper labor disputes that stem from changes in corporate structure and technology see A. H. Raskin, "The Big Squeeze on Labor Unions," *The Atlantic* (October 1978), pp. 41–48.

27. *Washington Post,* May 25, 1978, p. D-14.

28. Harold Trimmer, "Mergers in Printing: Why and Where They Are Happening," *Printing Production* (January 1970), p. 44, cited in Gregory Giebel, "Corporate Structure, Technology, and the Printing Industry," *Labor Studies Journal* (winter 1979), p. 238. Discussion of commercial printing is based largely on the Giebel article.

29. Solomon Blum, "Trade-Union Rules in the Building Trades," in *Studies in American Trade Unionism (1912),* eds. Jacob Hollander and George Barnett (New York: August Kelley, 1970), pp. 296–97.

30. E.g., Robert Christie, *Empire in Wood: A History of the Carpenters' Union* (Ithaca: Cornell University Press, 1956).

31. Jack Fuller, "Construction Unions Fighting for Survival in Philadelphia," *Washington Post,* July 4, 1972, p. A-8.

32. *Wall Street Journal,* July 7, 1972, p. 1.

33. *Washington Post,* April 8, 1978, p. A-1; *Wall Street Journal,* April 11, 1979, p. 40.

34. Rank-and-file bricklayers, who do not ratify local contract settlements, resisted the cuts. One of them articulated the traditional worker argument for a union policy that maximizes the wage bill independent of the effect on employment: "Maybe if there are 5,000 bricklayers and the business can only support 3,000, maybe 2,000 should get out. But at least let the 3,000 support themselves." Jerry Flint, "Bricklayers Protest Pay Cut in Contract," *New York Times,* January 8, 1978, p. 29.

35. *Washington Post,* April 8, 1978, p. A-1.

36. E.g., Gerace Construction, Inc. and Helger Construction Company, Inc., 193 NLRB 645 (1971); Peter Kiewit & Sons and South Prarie Construction Co., 206 NLRB 66 (1973).

37. "If You Can't Beat 'Em, Buy 'Em," *Forbes,* February 20, 1978, p. 46.

38. U.S. Congress, House, *Oversight Hearings on the National Labor Relations Act,* pp. 337–38. Seven different international unions lost their local union certifications in these 15 plants.

39. E. B. Barnes, "Why Salaried Operations," (Mimeo, no date), p. 2.

40. E.g., Dow Chemical Company, 227 NLRB No. 153 (1977); and the following cases: 81 LRRM 2872; 87 LRRM 1279; 88 LRRM 1622; 88 LRRM 1625; 86 LRRM 1381; 90 LRRM 3281; 91 LRRM 2275.

41. In 1974 the steelworkers union, which is the strongest and largest labor organization active in the chemical industry today, struck Dow's Midland, Michigan, plant for 176 days over economic issues. The stoppage had no visible adverse effects on Dow. The company kept the plant, which is its biggest facility, operating throughout the strike with some 2200 salaried employees. Dow's reported profits for the six-month period encompassing the walkout were higher than in the preceding half-year. The union failed to win its major bargaining objective, an open-ended cost-of-living clause, and instead made concessions in negotiated pension benefits. Of particular damage to the steelworkers and other chemical industry unions was the subsequent use of this unsatisfactory settlement as the chemical industry pattern in that year's round of bargaining. See "Dow Little Setback from Strike," *Chemical Week*, March 27, 1974, p. 15; "Work Goes On at Dow's Embattled Plant," *Chemical Week*, August 24, 1974, p. 51; "Dow Setting Pay Pattern," *Chemical Week*, September 18, 1974, p. 20.

42. *Wall Street Journal*, June 26, 1979, p. 7.

43. U.S. Congress, House, *Oversight Hearings on the National Labor Relations Act*, pp. 791–803.

44. *Florida Steel Corporation*, 226 NLRB No. 25 (1976).

45. See, for example, *Mosher Steel Company*, 226 NLRB No. 180 (1976).

46. *Steel Labor*, April 1978, p. 7.

47. *Wall Street Journal*, May 2, 1978, p. 48.

48. *Pittsburgh Press*, May 1, 1978, A-1.

49. *Wall Street Journal*, December 17, 1976, p. 13; April 19, 1976, p. 18; September 15, 1977, p. 8.

50. See the following Mueller Brass Company (Fulton, Miss.) cases: 204 NLRB No. 105 (1973); 208 NLRB No. 76 (1974); 220 NLRB No. 174 (1975).

51. *Federal Pacific Electric Co.*, 203 NLRB No. 93 (1973).

52. *Federal Pacific Electric Co.*, 215 NLRB No. 158 (1974).

53. *Centre* (County Pa.) *Daily Times*, March 6, 1978, p. 1.

54. "Bearing Imports To Go Down, Prices Up," *Purchasing* (February 5, 1974); *Iron Age*, April 29, 1974, p. 32.

55. Federal Mogul Corporation, 203 NLRB No. 156 (1973); Timkin Company, 213 NLRB No. 68 (1974). For a discussion of the human cost involved in shutting down Federal Mogul's Detroit plant, including at least seven suicides among the more than two thousand displaced production workers, see Don Stillman, "The Devastating Impact of Plant Relocations," *Working Papers* (July/August 1978): 42–53.

56. U.S. Congress, House, "Public Hearing on the Proposed Tender Offer to the Copperweld Corporation By Société Imetal," Subcommittee on Labor Standards of the Committee on Education and

Labor, House of Representatives, 94th Cong., 1st Sess. (Washington, D.C.: GPO, 1975), p. 5.

57. *Wall Street Journal,* December 3, 1975, p. 4; *McKeesport* (Pa.) *Daily News,* February 22, 1978, p. 1; March 1, 1978, p. 1; April 26, 1978, p. 1.

58. For example, see Charles Craypo, "Collective Bargaining in the Conglomerate, Multinational Firm: Litton's Shutdown of Royal Typewriter," *Industrial and Labor Relations Review* (October 1975): 1–25.

59. A more detailed discussion of these cases is in U.S. Congress, House, *Oversight Hearings on the National Labor Relations Act,* pp. 125–39.

60. *Ibid.,* pp. 135–36.

61. Gradually the NLRB has moved from its initial position of permitting employee free choice in bargaining-unit determination, substituting a history of bargaining criteria which preserve existing structures against either fragmentation or consolidation as a result of employee self-determination elections; see George Brooks and Mark Thompson, "Multi-plant Units: The NLRB's Withdrawal of Free Choice," *Industrial and Labor Relations Review* (April 1967). The inter-city bus industry offers an important example. The NLRB refuses to allow Trailways drivers to vote whether to be represented by a single bargaining agent in one unit covering Greyhound drivers, who, as a result of the differential in union bargaining strength between the two companies, enjoy substantially higher wages and benefits than those negotiated by two unions in numerous separate units at Trailways. Charles Craypo, "Bargaining Units and Corporate Merger: NLRB Policy in the Intercity Bus Industry."

62. Charles Lindblom, *Politics and Markets: The World's Political-Economic Systems* (New York: Basic Books, 1977), p. 176.

63. "Bearing Specialists Survey 70s," *Industrial Distribution* (June 1972): 46.

64. *SKF Industries, et al.,* Complaint Docket No. 9046, *FTC Complaints and Orders* (20961), July 22, 1975.

65. *Wall Street Journal,* March 26, 1979, p. 30; *Washington Post,* April 17, 1976.

66. George Brooks, *The Sources of Vitality in the American Labor Movement* (Ithaca: NYSSLIR, Cornell University, 1960).

67. Larry Mishel, "Corporate Structure and Bargaining Power: The Coordinated Bargaining Experience," *Labor Studies Journal* (winter 1979).

The Best Defense Is a Good Defense: Toward a Marxian Theory of Labor Union Structure and Behavior

David M. Gordon

> Much research has been carried out to trace the different historical phases that the bourgeoisie has passed through, from the commune up to its constitution as a class.
>
> But when it is a question of making a precise study of strikes, combinations, and other forms in which the proletarians carry out before our eyes their organization as a class, some [observers] are seized with real fear and others display a *transcendental disdain.*
>
> Karl Marx
> *The Poverty of Philosophy*

LABOR UNIONS ARE capturing increasing public attention throughout the advanced capitalist world. Do union wage gains cause inflation? Do organized workers impede the quest for greater productivity? Should there be a social contract? Do "right-to-work" laws undercut workers' relative power?

As these issues proliferate, many different interest groups have converged on some obvious questions:

What internal factors influence the relative strength and unity of trade unions? What frames the relationship between union members and union leadership? What are the respective interests and objectives of the rank and file and the leadership? How do unions conceive and execute their decisions and activities: How, in short, *do unions work?*

One would logically turn to social scientists for help with these questions. But the cupboard has been bare. Given the importance of labor unions in advanced capitalist countries, it is striking how underdeveloped the available literature on labor unions has remained. Both the mainstream and Marxian cupboards have shared this emptiness.

On the mainstream side the literature on labor unions has suffered from absentminded neglect. As George Johnson noted in a recent survey of the labor economics literature on unions (1975:23), close to 10 percent of articles (in leading U.S. economics journals) "dealt with union topics" in the 1940s, but that measure of relative attention has dropped continually since then: to 5.1 percent in the 1950s, 2.3 percent in the 1960s, and a trifling 0.4 percent during the early 1970s. This small and declining literature has focused primarily on the *impact* of trade unions on wages, prices, employment, and inequality, eliding questions of union structure and behavior almost completely.[2] Many factors might explain this inattention to union behavior and structure, of course, but it would certainly be sufficient to ascribe it to the lack of a determinate *theory* of unions as organizations. As Johnson himself concludes (1975:23–24), "the problem of modeling trade union behavior has proved to be virtually intractable. ... The absence of a solid theoretical foundation has handicapped the economic analysis of trade unions and has surely contributed to its decline in relative attention."

Traditional Marxian analyses of trade unions provide little more illumination of union behavior and structure. As Sidney Peck (1979) recently noted, 50 years have passed since progressives first responded to and began debating Selig Perlman's *A Theory of the Labor Movement* (1928). For almost those full 50 years Marxists have failed to move beyond the classic Marxian texts and the adopted insights from scholars like Perlman and John R. Commons. Almost the entire corpus of Marxian literature has focused on political (or "normative") questions: How should revolutionaries relate to the union movement? What contributions should unions make to the struggle for socialism? Behavioral (or "positive") analysis has correspondingly suffered. As Richard Hyman concludes in his recent review of the traditional Marxian literature on unions (1971: 53; emphasis in the original), "no *general* theory is available to relate the struggle for material reforms to the development of consciousness."[3]

So we must essentially start from scratch. Where to begin?

Almost all of the available literature agrees that unions' relative *power* in both collective bargaining and the political process plays a significant role in determining economic outcomes and unions' ability to advance their members' interests. Most analysts stop there, however, treating union power as an *exogenous* or *independent* variable, determined by factors lying outside of their own frames of reference. If we want to advance our understanding of labor unions, it seems critical to treat unions' power and behavior as *dependent* variables—as outcomes of politicoeconomic processes worthy of coherent and sustained analysis.

What determines union power? It seems obvious, as a way of mapping strategy for analysis, that both *external* and *internal* factors are likely to influence unions' power: both environmental determinants like the structure of their industries and the state of the economy; and internal forces like the militancy of their membership and the skills of their leaders. The greatest lacuna in the available literature involves its inattention to internal determinants of union power; this suggests that we should probably place higher priority on the exploration of these internal factors until that imbalance is redressed.

Unions are organizations comprising rank-and-file members, union officials,[4] and institutional rules and procedures. In order to "model" union structure and behavior, one needs to analyze the interactive relationships among these three union elements. That requires attention to a set of initially separable questions:

(1) What factors determine rank-and-file members' interests and capacity to pursue those interests?

(2) What factors determine union officials' interests and capacity to pursue them?

(3) What determines internal institutional rules and procedures and how do those organizational practices affect (a) the relationship between members and officials, (b) their respective interests, and (c) their respective capacities to advance those interests?

This essay seeks to establish a provisional Marxian analysis of these internal questions about labor union structure and behavior. The essay has three sections. The first provides a brief review of the traditional literature on labor unions and the sources of the weakness of that literature. The second section outlines my provisional theoretical model of labor union structure and behavior in capitalist economies.[5] (Since the available literature provides so little help along these dimensions, I want to emphasize in advance how tentatively I offer the analytic suggestions of this section.) The final section both reviews some of the limitations of that provisional model and summarizes its implications for further research and for political approaches to labor unions as organizations.

Traditional Economics Literature

With appropriate apologies to social scientists in other disciplines, I have concentrated in this section on the three main traditions of "labor economics": neoclassical, institutionalist, and Marxian analyses.[6] While hoping to appropriate help from the traditional literature wherever possible, I have also tried to highlight the sources of its incompleteness as a way of charting a path for transcending the principal limitations of that literature.

Neoclassical Analyses[7]

Some neoclassical economists have attempted to explore some of the questions with which this essay is concerned. Despite their primary attention to unions' impact, they have occasionally explored the determinants of unions' aggregated "preferences" about economic variables and have also modeled unions' propensity to strike.

All of these analyses begin by treating some important behavioral phenomena as fixed, as exogenously determined. The most important of these fixed institutional characteristics include: (a) internal union decision-making structure and rules, (b) aspects of production which might influence rank-and-file members' interests and relative power, (c) political traditions within and outside unions which might influence their orientation and relative militancy, and (d) the established legal and institutional procedures and requirements conditioning relationships with corporations and the government. Most analyses also take for granted the structure of the industry in which a union operates and the level at which collective bargaining takes place, although Hendricks (1975) has provided one interesting analysis of the effects of bargaining structure on unions' wage impact.

Given those fixed institutional structures, a few neoclassical economists have advanced some specific analytic propositions about unions' preferences and union strike activity:

Several analysts, including especially Ashenfelter and Johnson (1969) and Atherton (1973), have hypothesized that unions will be relatively more likely to engage in strikes (or other militant actions) if there are competing political factions within the union, if there are democratic and relatively frequent elections for leadership, and if the union's percentage membership share within a company or industry has been declining.

Some, particularly Ashenfelter and Johnson (1969) and Shorey (1976), have focused on several critical macroeconomic variables, suggesting that union members are especially likely to promote militant union demands (supported by strikes if necessary) if there have recently been relatively rapid increases in the aggregate level of prices and in either industry-specific or economywide rates of profit, if there have recently been relatively slow (or decelerating) increases in industry-specific real wages (among all production workers or members of the collective bargaining unit), and/or if there have recently been relatively low rates of unemployment.

Shorey (1976) has also emphasized that a few institutional variables may also influence strike activity, stipulating that strikes will vary directly with the prevalence of piece-rate wage systems and with the size of work units (or establishments) among industries.

Like institutionalist economists (see below), neoclassical labor economists have typically observed and/or hypothesized that rank-and-file union members are more likely to demand militant union practice than union leaders are likely to deliver it. These observations frame a corollary hypothesis—whose analytic foundations are rarely articulated—that union leaders are much more likely than rank and filers to cooperate with management and to prefer cooperative bargaining practice over sharp confrontations. As unions become more and more bureaucratic in their structures, neoclassical economists therefore propose the further hypothesis that unions will become "more 'responsible' in their dealings with management, to be more cautious in the use of the strike, more temperate in their public utterances, and perhaps less extreme in their demands." (Rees, 1962: 200) This observation sometimes leads to the corresponding and somewhat colored imputation of a contrast between the "maturity" of leadership and the "immaturity" of membership. As Rees put it (1962: 200), "the occasional revival of the exuberant, irresponsible unionism of the past depends largely on the possibility of occasional revolt by the rank and file."

None of this adds very much to our understanding of the determinants of internal union structure and behavior. We seek to explain and analyze exactly what neoclassical analysis either ignores or treats as an exogenously determined independent variable. Neoclassical analysts would explore the *impact* of relatively democratic procedures within a union, for example, while I would hope to be able to understand why and how and where such procedures emerge.

These elisions are typical of neoclassical analysis more generally. Abba Lerner once observed that economics "has gained the title of queen of the social sciences by choosing *solved* political problems as its domain." (Lerner, 1972: 259; emphasis in the original.) Neoclassical economics has traditionally examined, in other words, relationships which existed within the context of institutions whose structure and power relationships were *not* subject to either challenge or intensive examination. Rees exemplified this tendency in *The Economics of Trade Unions* (1962). He reserves questions of union structure for a chapter on "The Union as a Political Institution." He begins that chapter apologetically, anticipating surprise that he bothers with such issues at all. "Since this is primarily a book about the economics of trade unions," he notes (1962:170), "a chapter on politics may seem out of place." As long as neoclassical economists presume such a sharp separation between politics and economics, it would be surprising if their analyses of labor unions provided much help in understanding the internal structure and behavior of labor unions as politicoeconomic organizations.

Institutionalist Analyses[8]

While we owe most of what we know about unions in the United States to labor economists working within the "institutionalist" tradition, institutionalists' work has been crippled by a curious kind of methodological schizophrenia.

(1) At the level of concrete, "positive" analysis, institutionalist economists have generated a rich and subtle literature of union structure and behavior. They have studied the factors affecting union success in organizing different groups of workers, the influence of employees' work-place connections on their success at unionization, the forces determining variations in the degree of union democracy, and the sources of differences in the orientation and relative power of union leadership. And yet, befitting their intellectual tradition, institutionalists have

typically refrained from generalizing beyond these specific analyses toward more general "positive" propositions. Their analyses have remained discrete and disconnected. We learn that unions *are* what they *are*, but we do not learn much about how unions might be different if their circumstances changed from the given conjecture. (Institutionalists could have profited from a neoclassical lesson in comparative statics.)

(2) One source of this analytic failure obviously involves the relative indeterminancy of the institutionalists' theoretical framework.[9] But another, probably more important, source of that failure apparently lies with institutionalists' inclinations at the more "normative" level of analysis. Institutionalists generally believe that social conflict must be moderated and that cooperative collective bargaining can help not only in smoothing the operations of capitalist economies but also in reducing threats to their continued existence. The classic institutionalist treatise by Kerr *et al., Industrialism and Industrial Man* (1960), clearly reveals this orientation.

Apparently as a consequence of this normative predisposition, institutionalists typically abandon the care and subtlety of their concrete investigations when they turn to generalizations about the trajectory of union development in industrial economies. Because they *want* unions to develop cooperative practices and to discipline their membership, institutionalists assert that *unions are always likely to and will continue to develop those preferred characteristics.* One of the best institutionalized studies of union development, Richard Lester's *As Unions Mature* (1958), reveals this orientation. In the first instance Lester states his premises and preferences clearly (1958:17):

By guiding workers' discontent into orderly channels for its relief and by competing with other organizations for the representation of workers' varied interests, unions perform a beneficial role in a democratic society. Unions, by aiding in the reconciliation of conflicting interests, contribute to constructive social change. Collective bargaining, ideally, is a mutual exploration of difference, based on the facts, and a willingness to be convinced and to compromise temporarily.

Hoping to see what he wants, Lester concludes theoretically (1958:107):

The direction of the drift of union internal development is unmistakable. . . . The processes of internal change develop long-run trends toward internal stability, centralization, and machine control; the processes of external integration encourage a long-range tendency toward accommodation, orderly and peaceful arrangements, and breadth and moderation.

Institutionalist analyses spread during the period of increasing union stability in the 1950s and early 1960s, helping promote the structures which facilitated that stability. When union behavior began to change in the late 1960s, turning to greater militancy and more frequent strikes, institutionalists must have been surprised. The strength of their preferences for stable and cooperative union practice had led them to analyses which predicted the inevitability of such practice. When their predictions began to suffer the embarrassment of increasingly "anomalous" union behavior, institutionalists seemed to be caught with their analytic pants down. Because they typically failed to draw theoretical connections between their discrete, positive analysis and their general, normatively tinged analyses of union direction, they made the mistake of assuming that what they observed at one time in one place would always become more and more pervasive.

Institutionalists had assured us, in short, that unions would continue to change in a determinate direction. Because they failed to study the relative importance of various forces which had helped generate those directions for a time, they provided us relatively little help in understanding why and how union structure and behavior changed and might continue to change. We can continue to *observe,* in the spirit of the institutionalist tradition, but their work does not provide the key to overcoming our problems in *understanding.*

Marxian Analyses[10]

Somewhat surprisingly, Marxian analyses have also largely failed to pursue the kinds of investigations which would help us answer the questions posed at the beginning of this essay. While Marxist analysts have long debated the implications of trade unions for the socialist struggle, they have explored the actual determinants of union structure and behavior much less consistently.

Most of the twentieth-century Marxian literature on unions had focused on issues of political strategy. As Hyman summarizes this literature (1971:1–2):

> The perspectives which socialist theorists have generated may be roughly divided into two categories: those approaches which discern significant revolutionary potential in trade union activity; and those which argue that such activity does not in itself facilitate (or even that it inhibits) the revolutionary transformation of capitalist society.

Referring back to the Webbs' classic on *Industrial Democracy* (1897), Hyman makes a comment about the British literature which bears a striking resemblance to Peck's comment on the U.S. literature cited in the introductory section above (Hyman, 1971:1): "Over seven decades have passed since the publication of *Industrial Democracy;* yet it is difficult to name any subsequent work with the breadth of vision and theoretical insight to stand beside the Webbs' pioneering study."

Those Marxists who have focused on the actual operations of labor unions have largely concentrated on the effect of unions (of various characteristics) on the consciousness of workers (in various situations). Unions have been understood to *mediate* the relationship between workers' conditions and their consciousness, but Marxists have rarely done the kind of work which would allow us to understand how variations in unions' structure and behavior themselves arise.

This elision probably derives from the intensity of the political debate within the Marxian tradition over the appropriate political approach to trade-union activity. Of those who argued that unions enhanced workers' socialist consciousness and of those who argued that unions impeded it, *all* cared relatively little for the importance of variations among unions in their structure and behavior; all unions were either for us or ag'in us. In the tradition of this debate unions appeared like a kind of "black box," with their internal workings and determinants hidden from view. The tradition debate focused on their "intrinsic" characteristics without ever pausing to pay much attention to the differences which mysteriously existed inside that black box.

Some Marxists have moved recently to the more dialectical position that unions can serve both to promote and to impede socialist consciousness—as Anderson puts it (1962:264), that "trade unions are dialectically both an opposition to capitalism and a component of it." This recent orientation provides the direct impetus for the questions posed at the beginning of this essay. If unions both support capitalism and oppose it, then the internal structure and operations of unions undoubtedly influence the combination of those two effects. Unions in which the membership develops relatively greater power, for example, are probably more likely to impede capitalist control over production than unions with relatively less rank-and-file power. But what factors influence the relative power of membership within different unions? What forces shape union structures (with their corresponding influence on membership power)?

Traditional Marxian analyses have suffered some problems paralleling those of neoclassical and institutional analyses. Neoclassicists have forged a sharp separation between economic activities and "unsolved" political problems, while institutionalists have operated schizophrenically at both positive and normative levels, failing to make connections between those two levels of their analysis. Similarly, Marxists have placed such disproportionate emphasis on issues of political strategy that they have tended to neglect the factors influencing the environment conditioning political alternatives. Almost uniquely among Marxist students of labor unions, Richard Hyman (1975) has moved beyond the boundaries of the traditional debate precisely through his efforts to trace some of the determinants of internal union structure and behavior.[11]

These elisions in the traditional Marxist literature are particularly disappointing. Neoclassical economists have tended to neglect labor unions because unions represent unwanted "imperfections" in market economies. Institutionalists tend to compress union behavior into the mold which their normative predispositions prefer. Marxian analysis has generally emphasized the importance of structural and dialectical analyses, as it always seeks to understand the origins of important institutional forces which others overlook. Labor unions clearly represent a fundamental institutional force in the continuing evolution and transformation of advanced capitalist countries. Questions about their structure and behavior ought to play a comparably fundamental role in Marxian investigations of advanced capitalism.

A Marxian Analysis of Labor-Union Structure and Behavior

This section outlines a foundation for a Marxian theory of labor-union structure and behavior.[12] Because of limitations in space and time, I have concentrated entirely on formulating some provisional hypotheses which, in my view, comprise a useful starting point for a Marxian theoretical approach. I have been forced to leave for subsequent work and others' contributions the necessary additional stage of elaboration and testing of these hypotheses.

As I have argued elsewhere (Gordon, 1980), Marxian analyses must operate at three (at least) different levels of abstraction. One level, the most abstract, concerns the influence of the logic and dynamics of a dominant *mode of production:* in our case, the capitalist mode of production. A second level, at an intermediate level of abstraction, focuses on the influence of the internal structure and dynamics of a given *stage of accumulation.* The third level, more concrete, examines the specific sources of variation which can be attributed to concrete (but still determinate) influences within that broader structural context. The following three parts of this section present hypotheses at these three analytic levels respectively.

The Capitalist Mode of Production

This section briefly sketches some hypotheses about the influence of the structure and contradictions of the capitalist mode of production on the character of the struggle between employers and employees. It argues that we cannot properly understand the complex character of labor unions as institutions unless we locate their origins in the social relations of capitalist production.

According to the Marxian framework the character of production in capitalist economies is shaped by the interaction of intercapitalist competition and capitalist/worker conflict.[13] These twin imperatives jointly channel the directions in which capitalists and workers attempt to pursue and fulfill their respective needs and objections. This suggests that we must "model" those respective needs and objectives carefully if we hope to identify the most general kinds of forces which affect labor-union structure and behavior.

Capitalists. Those who seek to accumulate capital through the production of surplus value must continually address two interrelated problems in production: the continual reduction of their costs of production and the maintenance of control over their workers. (See Marglin, 1974; Gintis, 1976; and Gordon, 1976).

Marxists have traditionally hypothesized that capitalists will seek to create and reproduce the conditions necessary for *abstract labor* as one necessary strategy for solving these related problems. The notion of abstract labor refers to the existence of regularized and reliable comparability among individual units of "concrete labor." Unless capitalists can compare the characteristics of different workers, they cannot form reliable expectations about their potential rates of surplus value (and, consequently, their expected rates of profit). This requirement of abstract labor continually forces capitalists to pursue standards by which workers' output and dependability can be assessed, mechanisms for reducing the variability and randomness of their performance, and so on.[14]

I would also hypothesize that capitalists must additionally seek to create and reproduce the conditions necessary for *atomized labor* in their efforts to solve problems in production. The notion of atomized labor refers to the continual reproduction of divisible, fragmented, isolated units of labor: workers who are continually separated from one another. Why is atomized labor necessary? Capitalists hire many workers in production. Their common conditions and working experiences are likely to create social relationships which can potentially constitute a source of strength in opposition to employers. The more that workers can forge social connections the greater is their potential resistance to capitalist exploitation. The more that capitalists can create conditions of atomized labor the greater is the potential rate of exploitation of an individual worker's labor and, correspondingly, the higher is the potential rate of exploitation within a given unit of production.[15]

These two hypotheses can be combined. Given the existence of the capitalist mode of production (including both capitalists' control over the means of production and an available wage-labor force), individual capitalists will always be pushed toward systems of production which increase the possibility of both *abstract* and *atomized* labor in production.

Workers. When we begin analytically by assuming the existence of the capitalist mode of production, we begin with the existence (among other conditions) of wage-labor: with a large group of people who have no other alternative (for survival) than selling their labor power for a wage. Those wage laborers who find employment immediately enter a process in which they act in actual or potential conflict with their employers. While workers would always prefer a relatively higher wage (for a given amount of labor input), employers would always prefer a relatively lower one. While employers would always prefer workers to exert more labor effort per hour (given the wage), workers would always prefer to exert relatively less.[16] Given these intrinsic conflicts, and given employers' continuing efforts to improve their potential leverage over workers, workers are continually forced to take actions which will augment their relative power to increase their wages and/or to reduce their working time (above necessary labor). This would indicate that workers in capitalist production units will always be driven, at a minimum, in directions which would best improve their ability to resist the imposition of conditions of abstract and atomized labor.[17]

I would hypothesize that workers in capitalist enterprises will always be pressured to resist abstract labor by creating conditions for (what I would call) *differentiable labor*. Capitalists' power over workers will be continually reduced to the degree that they cannot make adjustments which render individual units of labor comparable to each other. It will therefore always be to workers' advantage, other things being equal, if they can differentiate the concrete characteristics of their units of labor power and labor activity.

I would further hypothesize that workers will always be pressured to resist atomized labor by creating conditions for (what I would call) *collective labor*. If capitalists can gain advantage by dissolving social connections among workers in production, then workers can presumably always improve their ability to resist capitalist exploitation by reestablishing and/or creating ties of collective solidarity which reduce employers' ability to manipulate individual workers and which forge unified action among as many employees as possible.

Abstract labor/differentiable labor//atomized labor/ collective labor . . . these are twin imperatives emerging from the structure and contradictions of capitalist production. For workers to create a regular and reproducible power to differentiate and collectivize their labor, they must establish some mechanisms which sustain and defend whatever gains they are able to achieve. I propose that we can refer generically to *labor unions* as the institutional mechanisms which workers create for these purposes. I would propose, in short, that labor unions in capitalist economies can be most clearly understood as *institutions which represent the composite outcome of workers' efforts to create conditions of both differentiable and collective labor.*

Conclusions. These hypotheses point toward three general conclusions about labor unions in capitalist economies (even before we proceed to the following two levels of analysis).

First, labor unions are by their nature potentially contradictory institutions. Workers' efforts to differentiate and to collectivize their labor may not always be compatible with each other. (Craft unions differentiate, for example, at the expense of maximum possible collective strength within a unit of production or industry.) Because labor unions as institutions must partly rigidify a set of connections among workers for the purposes of sustaining those connections, this process of rigidification may sometimes leave workers short of the best available potential combination of differentiation and collectivization. As the character of the demand for labor in capitalist economies changes, for example, workers' strength may lose some of the power which differentiation had formerly provided them. The only possible ultimate resolution of the immanent contradictions between the imperatives of differentiable and collective labor would come when all workers in the entire global capitalist system have been united in one cohesive collective force. Short of that final moment, workers and their unions will always face complicated and potentially contradictory choices between emphasis on relative differentiation of their labor from others and relative collectivization with others. (The historic debates between craft and industrial unions and the more recent debates over tariff policies and runaway shops both reflect this immanent tension.[18])

Second, this set of propositions about the origins of trade unions in capitalist economies can also help clarify the source of the traditional socialist debates about strategies toward labor unions. Some socialists have traditionally emphasized the necessity of trade-union struggle. Others have traditionally emphasized the futility and shortsightedness of trade-union struggle. (See Hyman, 1971, for a summary of these traditional positions.) The previous theoretical propositions obviously suggest that *both* emphases are correct.

On the one hand, workers will always want to increase their wages (and improve working conditions) and/or to reduce the surplus labor time they exert in the service of capitalists' profits. Because capitalists will always seek atomized and abstract labor, workers will *always* have to pursue trade-union power in order to increase their ability to pursue their needs and objectives within capitalist production. Trade-union action toward differentiable and collective labor, from this theoretical starting point, is inescapably necessary for workers in capitalist enterprises.[19]

On the other hand, these theoretical hypotheses began with the assumption of the *prior* existence of the capitalist mode of production—and consequently with the twin assumptions of capitalists' controlling the means of production and workers' being "doubly free" to sell their labor power for a wage. The conceptualization of labor unions therefore begins with workers in a defensive position, subordinate to capitalists as long as capitalists can reproduce their basic control of the means of production. Trade unions can only become offensive weapons, through which workers can fundamentally seize and sustain the initiative, if workers can pose a fundamental challenge to capitalists' control of the means of production.[20] By definition this would involve a transformation of the conditions within which we have postulated the origins of trade unions. For trade unions to become effective offensive weapons, in short, it would be necessary for workers to transcend the conditions which define and shape trade-union action: to transform their unions into something that they are not. Until they achieve the power to do so, workers must rely on trade unions as nothing more than defensive weapons. Short of an end to workers' subordination to capital, our postulates highlight the most obvious approach to labor union activities: *The best defense is a good defense.*

Third, these theoretical hypotheses by themselves can serve as a basis for clarifying the differences among neoclassical, institutionalist, and Marxian approaches to labor unions at the most abstract level. Neoclassical analysts are inclined to view capitalist economies as potentially harmonious systems, as structural mechanisms capable of providing the basis for mutual benefit among all economic participants within those structures. This leads them to view unions as either unnecessary or intrusive: unnecessary because free exchange will promote the maximum benefit for individual workers (without the help of unions, thank you very much!) and/or intrusive because unions are likely to interfere with the free and unconstrained individual exchange which best supports maximum mutual benefit. Institutionalists acknowledge the continual recurrence of conflict between capitalists and workers in capitalist economies but view labor unions (and collective bargaining procedures) as institutions best suited to the moderation of those conflicts. While unions may sometimes tend to promote conflict, institutionalists argue that they *should* seek to reduce it. In sharp contrast, Marxists would argue that unions are created and continually influenced by intrinsic conflicts between capitalists and workers, that they are ultimately workers' defense mechanisms through which they seek protection against capitalists' power, and, therefore, that unions are ultimately incapable of achieving a stable moderation of the conflicts which capitalist production generates. If unions try to play that role for a sustained period of time, they are likely to encounter serious and sustained opposition from the members whose objectives they seek to trim. Whatever the political strategies which Marxists politically adopt toward labor unions, Marxist theory would project that unions will, in "the last instance," be dominated by their function as mechanisms promoting the protective differentiation and collectivization of workers' labor in capitalist economies.

Stages of Accumulation

I have recently formalized and extended the Marxian theory of stages of accumulation. (See Gordon, 1980.)

This theory suggests that a stable and reproducible "social structure of accumulation" is a necessary condition for rapid capital accumulation, that various institutional requirements must be fulfilled in order for capitalists to be able to launch and sustain their quest for ever-increasing profits. (Reliable labor-market structures must exist, for example, for employers to be able to secure the labor power they need for production.) These successive social structures of accumulation frame the development of corporate and worker activities and strategies. As the environment for capital accumulation changes from one stage to the next, the limits to and possibilities for trade-union structure and behavior obviously change. This suggests that there can be no completely *general* Marxian theory of labor-union structure and behavior. Rather, it indicates that we must provide separate analyses of union structure and behavior for each successive stage of accumulation.[21]

There is another aspect to the theory of stages of accumulation which also has important implications for the analysis of union structure and behavior. I have hypothesized some connections between stages of accumulation and long economic cycles (Gordon, 1980), arguing that tendencies toward the instability of accumulation and toward economic crisis create the dissolution of one social structure of accumulation and require the constitution of a successor. This connection between stages of accumulation and long economic cycles leads me to postulate that each stage of accumulation can be viewed as passing through five phases—each with a different rhythm flowing from the changing dynamics of accumulation. (See Gordon, 1980, for further detail.) This leads, in turn, to the further hypothesis that systemic pressures on labor-union structure and behavior will change systematically from one *phase* of a stage of accumulation to the next. In the following paragraphs I briefly sketch the internal dynamics of the five phases and then delineate some specific hypotheses about the differential impact of those respective phases on union structure and behavior. After each hypothesis I provide an example which illustrates (but obviously does not test) that hypothesis.[22] (Most of the examples, because of limits to my own knowledge, involve the United States.)

Phase A. At the beginning of each stage of accumulation the new social structure of accumulation is put into place. Social struggles over power and social relationships begin to acquire a definitive resolution. Institutional relationships are established.

This phase will, therefore, also involve the formalization of some provisional relations of *accommodation* between labor unions and corporations. Were labor unions not to accept certain limits on their efforts to increase workers' relative power, there would be little possibility for the stabilization of institutions necessary to permit the restoration of accumulation. This phase is therefore likely to create two important kinds of effects. Hypotheses: (1) There are likely to be very strong pressures on labor unions to accept limits to their prerogatives, to accept an accommodation to some of the basic facts of life (including capitalists' domination of production) in capitalist economies. (As an example, between 1942 and 1950 in the U.S., pressures grew on industrial unions to accept basic collective bargaining parameters, including "management prerogative" clauses; to control their militants; and to exclude radicals from their ranks.) (2) Many within labor unions are likely to perceive some obvious advantages to accommodation in order to stabilize their own bureaucratic power and to consolidate whatever gains have emerged for them from the previous crisis. (As an example, Samuel Gompers moved rapidly toward craft-union accommodation with big business, including membership in the National Civic Federation, precisely during those years from 1898 to 1903 when the institutions of the new stage of accumulation in the United States were first acquiring shape.)

Phase B. After a social structure of accumulation is put into place, a period of rapid accumulation — what Marxists sometimes call stable expanded reproduction — takes place. Social relationships hold together, prosperity spreads, and economic stability prevails.

Hypotheses: (1) Because of the generality of prosperity, it is likely that many trade unions will be able to bargain for and successfully win tangible increases in real wages and significant improvements in working and living conditions. (As an example, real wages rose rapidly and industrial accident rates declined steadily for U.S. union members from the early 1950s through the mid-1960s.) (2) If and when there are differences in the relative bargaining power of different groups of workers — both within the organized sector and between organized and unorganized workers — inequalities in working and living conditions among those different groups of workers are likely to spread. (As an example, income inequalities between organized and unorganized workers in the United States appear to have increased between the late 1940s and the mid-1960s.) (3) Assuming that the most powerful sectors of the union movement are likely to achieve many of their objectives through bargaining during this period, it is likely (a) that organizing activity will slow (because of greater inclination toward strategies of "differentiable" labor), (b) that strike activity will decline, and (c) that union's share of the labor force will increase less rapidly or actually decline. (As an example, all three of these tendencies were apparently manifest in the United States not only during the 1950s and early 1960s but also during the period from about 1903 through the beginning of World War I.)

Phase C. Eventually, as tendencies toward economic instability become increasingly manifest, there is a deceleration of the rate of accumulation. The margin for reproducing the previous rates of growth in both profits and workers' wages begins to narrow.

Hypotheses: (1) This phase is therefore likely to lead to spreading strike activity as workers seek to protect the previous rates of increase in their real wages. (As an example, Cronin [1980] documents that strike activity in Britain has intensified during this phase of the long cycle in each successive stage of accumulation.) (2) As margins for accommodation narrow, those groups with the least bargaining power are increasingly likely to engage in relatively explosive protest; since they lack more organized instruments to protect their interests, they must turn to more aggressive strategies. (As an example, civil rights movements among blacks in the United States became more aggressive during this phase about the time of the Civil War, about World War I, and during the mid-1960s.) (3) Compared to other phases when protest also seems likely (see below), workers' and union protests during this phase are likely to be relatively "economistic," focusing on demands over wages and working conditions, paying relatively less attention to more basic questions of economic and political organization and power. (As an example, although strikes spread in the United States during the mid- and late-1960s, they focused much less on organizing issues than did strikes of the 1930s.)

Phase D. If and when the stagnation of accumulation continues, it begins to create spreading *institutional* uncertainty and instability. Both corporations and unions continue to act as if their problems can be solved on the basis of the instruments of the *prior* period of stable prosperity, but instability and competition create mounting difficulty for the pursuit of those strategies.

Hypotheses: (1) Because instability is spreading but unions have not yet begun to attack the sources of that instability, rising unemployment and institutional instability are likely to reduce unions' relative bargaining strength (compared, at least, to phases B and C); this is likely to lead to temporary weakness and declining strike activity. (As an example, strike activity declined dramatically in the late 1920s and stayed low in the early 1930s; it also appears to have remained surprisingly low in the early 1970s.) (2) As a result of this first tendency, rank-and-file members are likely to become increasingly restive with their current arrangements and union leaders and to begin to press toward changes in institutional relationships; if they are unionized, this is likely to create substantial rank-and-file pressure on union leadership. (As an example, informal work-group activity appears to have increased in the U.S. during the 1920s, and rank-and-file insurgencies against union leadership appear to have increased during the 1970s.)

Phase E. When crisis finally strikes, it becomes increasingly apparent to both capitalists and workers (as well as other groups) that the resolution of crisis requires activities and struggles with an increasingly *structural* orientation—activities aimed, that is, at the structural framework which frames individual activity.

Hypotheses: (1) Unions are likely to push for changes in the social context affecting their relative power. (As an example, as the Depression wore on, unions intensified their pressures for legislation strengthening workers' right to unionize.) (2) Workers are also likely to "innovate" in their struggles in order to achieve broader effect and to overcome the barriers to unity posed by labor-market competition and high unemployment. (As an example, workers relied increasingly on mass, "spontaneous" demonstrations in the late 1880s and workers "invented" the "sit-down" after 1935.) (3) Once these first two conditions are fulfilled, workers' protest is likely to spread rapidly, with strike activity increasing until well into the beginning of the next stage of accumulation. (As an example, strikes increased rapidly in the U.S. from the mid-1880s through 1903 and again from 1936 through the late 1940s; Cronin [1980] shows the same pattern for English strike activity.)

Conclusions. These hypotheses suggest two additional general guidelines for the development of a Marxian analysis of union structure and behavior.

First, this analysis indicates that one should not seek a single general and encompassing theory of union structure and behavior in capitalist economies. While we have already seen that there are some relatively general determinants of the character of union activity—flowing from the imperatives toward differentiable and collective labor—it also seems obvious that intermediate determinants of union structure and behavior will change from one stage of accumulation to the next. There are likely to be important variations, moreover, in the form of specific institutions *among* countries *within* a given stage of accumulation. (Although some aspects of the post-World War II period were common among the advanced countries, for example, there were some important differences in the institutions framing emergent collective bargaining policy among those countries.)

Second, this analysis also suggests that one should

probably avoid the quest for mechanical hypotheses about secular tendencies in the character of union activities over time. An earlier generation of institutionalists hypothesized a continuous secular decline in union strike activity, for example. (See especially Ross and Hartman, 1960.) The eruption of strike activity in the late 1960s appeared to confute their hypotheses. (See Crouch and Pizzorno, 1978.) Both observations were provisional, however, since a more general historical view seems to suggest that union strike activity will be concentrated in phases C and E of the long cycle and that our impressions of strike activity will themselves depend on the phase of the long cycle within which we make our own observations.[23] (See Cronin, 1980.)

Concrete Variations within Stages of Accumulation

However useful these initial hypotheses may seem, they represent only a beginning. They suggest that both the logic and contradictions of capitalist production in general and the logic and dynamics of stages of accumulation will have important infuence on the structure and behavior of labor unions. Given capitalism and given an existing stage of accumulation, however, there are undoubtedly many additional factors which help shape union structure and behavior. I present in the following paragraphs a sequence of hypotheses at a relatively more concrete level of analysis. These hypotheses can serve as a kind of check list for additional influences which may condition labor-union activities. As in the preceding section, I identify specific hypotheses and follow them with illustrative examples.

Determinants of Rank-and-File Activity and Relative Power.
Since workers' activities ultimately give rise to labor

unions in the first place, it seems most useful to begin with determinants of rank-and-file workers' activities toward labor unions and their relative power within those institutions.

(1) Workers' inclinations toward and activities within labor unions will be affected *by the character and strength of their basic social connections at the level of "informal work groups."*[24] (For the purposes of the discussion which follows, I define an informal work group as the smallest irreducible nexus of direct, unmediated social connections among workers within a unit of production. For more on informal work groups from a management perspective see Sayles, 1954.)

(a) If basic informal work groups are too small, workers will not develop a strong sense of collectivity and will be likely to lag in their efforts to push for strong union representation and effective rank-and-file representation within their unions. (As an example, since the basic informal work group for truckers is the single truck driver alone in a cab, it is not surprising that rank-and-file activity within the Teamsters Union has often been relatively muted.)

(b) If informal work groups are of reasonable size and social connections among workers emphasize interdependence, it is likely that workers' inclination toward collective union action and rank-and-file activity in the union will be relatively strong. (As an example, given the interconnections among workers established by the assembly line, it is not surprising that autoworkers helped pioneer the sit-down strike and continued to manifest rank-and-file action even after UAW leadership began to try to calm such action. See Bernstein, 1971; and Lichtenstein, 1979).

(c) If technical or social changes in production either diminish (or increase) the strength or intensity of relations among workers within their informal work groups, these changes are likely to produce corresponding diminutions (or intensifications) in the strength and militancy of workers' rank-and-file activity toward and within their unions. (As an example, oil workers report that rank-and-file strength in their union declined substantially after the institution of automatic valves "stretched out" workers' stations along the pipelines to such great distances that workers lost physical contact with each other during much of the working day.)

(d) Since informal work-group connections constitute the *foundation* for rank-and-file strength within unions, struggles for union democracy will significantly advance the power of rank and file if and to the degree that workers protect and strengthen social connections within informal work groups. (As an example, organizers in the phone company report that local union strength hinges critically on maintaining and sustaining connections within informal work groups and that company supervisors continually rotate workers from one "shop" to another in order at least partly to break up strong informal groups.)

(2) The degree of homogeneity among jobs and workers within units of production is likely to have important impact on the solidarity and relative strength of rank-and-file activity within unions.

(a) The greater the degree of job differentiation within informal work groups, the greater the likelihood of weakened rank-and-file activity. (As an example, one common observation about barriers to white-collar unionism in many industries focuses on the relatively greater degree of job differentiation and vertical hierarchy *within* office units. See Lockwood, 1958.)

(b) The greater the degree of status or occupational

differentiation *among* informal work groups *within* collective bargaining units, the lower the likelihood of unified rank-and-file solidarity and, therefore, the lower the likelihood of rank-and-file power within a union. (As an example, it is at least a plausible observation that the reduced constitutional and actual lower levels of rank-and-file formal and actual power within the United Steelworkers of America, compared to other large U.S. industrial unions, derives at least partly from the long and deep historical roots of highly differentiated job ladders and "ports-of-entry" in basic steel production. On the early roots of these structures see Stone, 1974.)

(c) The greater the degree of heterogeneity (in the characteristics of production) within a union, the greater the barriers to effective rank-and-file unity and influence within that union structure. (As an example, the vast gulf in working conditions between light electrical assembly and heavy electrical production [like turbine production] probably helps explain some of the fragmentation between unions representing electrical workers in the United States.)

(d) Along any or all of these (three preceding) dimensions—within informal workgroups, among informal work groups, and among units of production— important cleavages among groups of workers with respect to race, sex, or cultural/national background will reduce rank-and-file workers' actual and potential strength within the union. (As an example, the distance and mutual suspicion between older Irish workers and younger black and Puerto Rican workers have clearly undercut rank-and-file strength in the New York City Transit Workers Union—after earlier decades of vigorous and militant rank-and-file activity.)

(3) The mechanisms through which workers in differ-

ent informal work groups *communicate with each other* are likely to have a fundamental impact on rank-and-file strength within a union.

(a) If workers who regularly move *among* informal work groups are also (i) within the collective bargaining unit and (ii) maintain regular production activities (instead of becoming paid union officials), they are likely to provide particularly effective rank-and-file leadership and to promote the voice of the rank and file within the union. (As an example, Strauss [1953] showed in one case study that the workers in a utilities company who were most actively inclined toward industrial unionism *and* contributed the most effective leadership were those whose jobs provided easy communication both within their shops and among shops within the company [1953:24]: "Thus, job characteristics played their part in determining which groups could become active in the union and from which groups the leaders of the new union would arise.")

(b) Rank-and-file strength in unions will hinge on the density of "front-line" union representatives—what are commonly called either shop stewards or shop committeemen/women. Other things equal, the higher the ratio of stewards or committee members to production workers—that is, the higher the "ratio of representation"—the greater the voice of the rank and file within the union. (As an example, many unions find it necessary periodically to remap patterns of representation after shifts in the relative size of shop units because rank-and-file workers complain about attrition in their representation.)

(c) The more that company foremen or supervisors supplant production workers or union reps as mechanisms of real communication among workers, the weaker will be rank-and-file influence within the union (because management will be appropriating and therefore monopolizing so much of rank-and-file communication). (As an example, many U.S. phone workers complain that there are so many supervisors per worker that they have difficulty establishing their own channels of independent communication.)

(d) We can combine hypotheses (3b) and (3c) into a more general and fundamental proposition about communication: Rank-and-file influence within unions will depend on what I have (somewhat playfully) called the "ratio of ratios": on the relationship between the relative density of management supervision and union representation. Suppose we measure these respective densities as simple continuous variables, denoting the density of company supervision by S_i / P_i and the density of union representation by C_i / P_i , where S measures the number of supervisors, C the number of stewards or committee reps, and P the number of production workers, while the subscript refers to specific production units within a given union. The ratio of ratios is then:

$$R_i = \frac{S_i / P_i}{C_i / P_i} = \frac{S_i}{C_i}, i = 1, 2, \ldots, n.$$

The higher the average R_i within a union or the more it increases over time, the weaker the rank and file is likely to be within the union. (As an example, apparently reflecting some of this logic, the United Autoworkers has recently made the "density of supervision," in my terms, a bargainable issue.)

(e) If rank-and-file workers develop a new and relatively independent mechanism for communicating among themselves as production workers, it is likely that they will increase their relative influence within their unions. (As an example, most observers agree that the spread of citizen-band radios among truck drivers, providing them with a dramatic increase in their capacity for self-communication and effectively creating "informal work groups" where they scarcely existed before, has played a central stimulating role in the increase in rank-and-file activity within the Teamsters Union in the U.S. since the early 1970s.)

(4)Rank-and-file activity within unions will also obviously depend on workers' attitudes—on their expectations about their working conditions, wages, and relative power.

(a) Rank-and-file activity will depend on the degree to which their working conditions exceed or fall under their *expectations* about the quality of their working conditions. The more their expectations exceed reality, other things equal, the more actively they will pursue their interests within the union. (As an example, dust conditions apparently did not intensify in U.S. coal mines in the 1970s, but workers' changing expectations about dust conditions and "black lung" disease clearly helped promote more intensive rank-and-file activity within the mineworkers union.)

(b) Workers do not protest over absolute wage levels as such, no matter how great their "money illusion," but they are likely to struggle over wage levels with respect to historically conditioned expectations, with respect to relative inequalities among different groups of workers, and with respect to relative rates of increase in real profits (and real wages). It seems likely, therefore, that workers will most actively push for higher wages in order to maintain recent rates of increase in real wages; if other, relatively comparable groups have recently received real wage increases; and/or if corporate or industry profits have recently been increasing rapidly. (As an example, New York City collective bargaining has been forced to contend for years with the sanctity of "parity" in salaries among the various uniformed workers — including especially police, fire, and sanitation.)

(c) Workers' expectations about their demands and their willingness to push for those demands will undoubtedly depend, to some degree, on the general state of economic activity and the level of relative demand for their labor. The tighter the labor market (in which workers sell their labor power), other things equal, the more likely that workers will expect that their activities in pursuit of their own interests will bear fruit and that workers will feel relative immunity from the razor's edge of the threat of dismissal and unemployment. (As an example, many labor economists have found some determinate relationship between the rate of unemployment and workers' propensity to strike, although the relationship is more complicated than sometimes believed. See, for example, Ashenfelter and Johnson, 1969.)

(d) Workers inherit workplace and union "cultures": standards and values which influence their perception of their conditions and what is due them. The greater the "collective" and "democratic" and/or "socialist" culture within a given workplace, other things equal, the more active and militant rank-and-file workers are likely to be within their union. (As an example, E. P. Thompson's classic study of the formation of the English working class [1967] illustrates the complexity *and* determinant importance of this kind of heritage.)

Determinants of Internal Union Structure. While rank-and-file activity by itself will play an important role in shaping the internal structure of unions, many other forces will have important influence as well. Union structures may vary along a wide variety of dimensions, including the right of members to ratify contracts, the level at which grievance procedures are determined, the salaries of leadership, the level at which collective bargaining negotiation takes place, the procedures for selecting leadership, and the general mechanisms (both formal and informal) through which members can seek to influence leaders (and vice versa). Many of these structural dimensions are likely to vary together. For that reason I have concentrated in this section on the general dimension of *the degree of centralism in union structure.* What factors, along many different dimensions, influence the degree to which union decisions and actions are charted by a relatively centralized leadership relatively immune from the direct influence and opinions of rank-and-file membership?

(1) Many dimensions of firm and industry structure and behavior will in turn affect the degree of centralism in a union.

(a) The larger the firm and/or the more "concentrated" an industry, other things equal, the more centralized will be union decision-making as a result of the requisites of collective bargaining. In order to be able to negotiate, unions have to be able to present and sustain coordinated and disciplined proposals. (As an example, based on what little I know, it would be plausible to argue that variations in the relative democracy and rank-and-file influence within municipal unions in the U.S. are associated inversely with the size of the city government with which they bargain.)

(b) The more heterogeneous is the industrial composition of a given union, the more likely it is that such a union will be forced to conduct bargaining on a relatively more decentralized level, that there will not be a developed central union strength, and/or that there will be frequent "fractional" bargaining within the union. (As an example, the Oil, Chemical, and Atomic Workers Union conducted bargaining at a plant level for many years; it may be that the industrial heterogeneity of the union's workers made it difficult for the union to develop the centralized strength which would have supported more centralized bargaining practices. On "fractional" bargaining see Hampton, 1967.)

(c) The more *indirect* or bureaucratic the corporate and industrial systems for labor management and the extraction of surplus value, the more centralized are union structures likely to become. If exploitation is mediated by shop-floor intensification of labor, unions are likely to be active at the shop-floor level. If exploitation is mediated through systems management, automation, and more centralized systems of information, unions will have to operate at those (more indirect) levels in order to pursue potential influence over the rate of surplus value. (As an example, companies actively sought during the 1950s and 1960s to settle grievances "off the shop floor" at relatively high levels of administrative management. This led in turn to relatively centralized systems for union processing of grievances.)

(d) The more interdependent are the production processes and the more that wages are tied to workers' productivity, the more directive will unions be of workers' labor effort and, therefore, the greater will be the potential opposition between rank-and-file membership and union leadership. (As an example, in many piece-rate systems, workers' wages are tied directly to their own individual efforts, and union protection of their wage levels does *not* require union mediation of their labor effort—although unions need to intervene to influence the piece-rate itself. In large-scale and capital-intensive industry, where collective bargaining over wages often revolves around the rate of increase in productivity, there is, in contrast, a strong tendency for unions to become monitors of individual units' work effort on behalf of the entire membership's aggregate rate of productivity increase.)

(2) The relative centralism of a union will also obviously depend on the relative strength, unity, and militancy of its rank-and-file membership.

(a) The more active the rank and file, other things being equal, the more likely it is that there will be provisions for rank-and-file ratification, recall, and frequent election of officers. (As an example, even though the garment industry is decentralized and populated with small firms, the historical relative weakness of the rank and file probably helps explain some of the relatively centralized internal procedures of the garment workers union in the U.S.)

(b) The greater is the inconsistency between rank-and-file pressure for union influence and external pressures toward centralist structures, the more likely it becomes that unions will develop dual (or several) structures of power, effecting a compromise between the push for democracy and the pressure for effective and coordinated bargaining. (As an example, both the steel industry and the auto industry are highly centralized in firm and industry structures, creating pressures toward centralized union leadership. In view of those similarities, it is apparently the greater unity of auto informal work groups, compared to the differentiation among informal work groups within the steel industry, which helps explain the emergence of a dual line of power in the UAW in the U.S. Rank and file elect their own committee reps and local union officers, in real and actively contested elections allocating determinant union power, while international and regional officials have much more influence over bargaining and the administration of grievance procedures. In the Steelworkers union, in contrast, there is no rank-and-file ratification on many issues, and local officials have much less autonomous power.)

Determinants of Leaders' Objectives and Behavior. Union leadership will not necessarily seek the same objectives as union membership. To a very large degree the similarity or dissimilarity of members' and leaders' objectives will flow from the relative strength of the rank and file and the relative democracy of union structures. These influences can be derived from the previous sections on rank-and-file activity and union structure. There is one additional set of potential influences on leaders' objectives which may operate relatively independently of those first two sets of determinants.

(1) The relative centrality of a given industry in the national economy and the relative importance of labor unions in established (and, particularly, "ruling") political parties will also affect the degree to which leaders weigh "national" factors alongside members' interests and may, indeed, place higher priority on the former.

(a) If a given industry occupies a critical role in the national economy, union leaders may experience intensive pressure from national leaders and may begin to develop a perspective on union demands which involves different priorities than members' own preferences. (As an example, national pressure on the coal miners' leadership during their recent strikes in the U.S., itself attributable to coal's economic importance, apparently had considerable influence on the compromises the leadership made during negotiations and therefore helps explain the narrow margin by which the rank and file approved the negotiated contract proposals.)

(b) If unions constitute an important block in a ruling political party whose positions depend on union support and advocacy, union leaders may place especially heavy influence on considerations of national impact and weigh the interest of nonunion members (whose support the political coalition seeks) at least as heavily as those of its own members. (As an example, the importance of unions within the ruling Swedish Social Democratic Party apparently helps explain the relative lack of rank-and-file influence over many union policies and an apparent [relatively recent] alienation of many union members from their leaders' policies.)

Conclusions. This very long list of hypotheses, however suggestive, accomplishes nothing more than sketch a theoretical framework within which relatively concrete Marxian analyses of union structure and behavior can be located. The general point should be obvious: there are a wide variety of factors, all of them more or less endogenous to the Marxian analysis of capitalist political economies, which condition variations in union structure and behavior. Before we can actually "explain" activities which unions undertake as institutions, I would argue that we must seek to trace the interaction *within* unions of members' preferences and capacities, union procedures and modes of operation, and leaders' preferences and activities. If we are to move beyond treatments of unions as "black boxes," we must trace the internal determinants of union structure and behavior along *all* of the dimensions hypothesized in the preceding paragraphs. Figure 1 traces the different directions of interaction among all the different sources of influence on union structure and behavior, indicating in particular that we can analyze union behavior only as an outcome of a complicated pattern of interdependent behavior.

Figure 1

THE PATTERN OF INFLUENCE ON UNION STRUCTURE AND BEHAVIOR

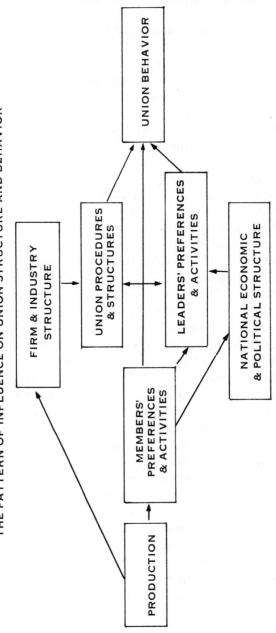

Implications of the Analysis

Because this essay is already so long, I prefer to conclude with some simple and brief comments on the potential implications of this initial theoretical effort.

First, this tentative exercise suggests to me the possibility of rapid and substantial progress toward a Marxian analysis of labor-union structure and behavior with three important characteristics: (1) The analysis can achieve a much greater degree of complexity than many earlier and traditional Marxian analyses seemed to provide. (2) At the same time such an analysis can achieve a rigor and determinacy not only in spite of but precisely because of its greater complexity. The more carefully we model the full range of influences on union structure and behavior, the more theoretical and empirical precision we can achieve. (3) While pursuing greater complexity and rigor, Marxian analyses can remain confident about the essential differences between our own and other economic perspectives on labor unions. Because a Marxian analysis can locate the origins of trade unions in a specific understanding of the contradictions of capitalist production, that analysis will inevitably build upon hypotheses about both the inevitability and the necessity of conflict within unions and between unions and management which neither mainstream nor institutionalist perspectives are likely to share.

Second, this provisional analysis suggests the need for a dramatic shift in research priorities. Most recent research on labor unions has focused on behavior *outcomes,* like strikes, and indices of unions' *impact* on variables like wages and employment. In order to understand how and why unions behave as they do, however, the analysis of this essay suggests that we must pay much more attention to (and collect data about) dimensions of internal union structure and behavior. We need much more information on (a) the links between the structure of production and the character of rank-and-file activities,[25] (b) the origins of and sources of variation in union structure and procedures,[26] and (c) analyses which link variations in leaders' preferences to those sources of influence (among others).[27]

Third, this essay suggests the need for a much more complex political approach to trade-union activity. Progressives have too often taken an all-or-nothing approach to labor unions. If there are as many independent sources of influence on union structure and behavior as this essay indicates, then there should be just as many relatively independent considerations affecting political approaches to unions. Depending on channels of communication among informal work groups, to pick only one example, strategies for promoting rank-and-file influence within unions will undoubtedly need to vary from one union to another precisely because means of access to those workers will vary. Failure to take these kinds of factors into account, I would fear, will fundamentally cripple the potential strength of both workers and their unions. If the best defense is a good defense, both players and coaches need to learn a great deal more about how the game works.

NOTES

1. Marx (1963: 173), emphasis in the original.

2. Mainstream economists have made one exception, studying the determinants of union behavior in the form of strikes. They are also beginning to study the impact of unions on production — particularly on productivity. See, for example, Brown and Medoff (1978).

3. For a useful compilation of recent Marxian work on unions see Clarke and Clements (1978).

4. For the purposes of this essay I provisionally define labor-union

officials as those who earn salaries from unions and/or get paid time-off from employers in order to perform union tasks. There can obviously be rank-and-file leaders and representatives who remain production workers and do not work as union officials.

5. I have limited the analysis to the structure and behavior of unions in *capitalist* economies partly because of the underdevelopment of Marxian analyses of societies in socialist transition and partly because I know so much less about those situations.

6. I have concentrated on the economics literature for two reasons. First, I know that literature much better than comparable materials from other disciplines. Second, many social scientists tend to regard economic analysis as more "rigorous" and "determinate" than that in other disciplines. If I can reasonably criticize the existing literature in economics because it is not determinate enough, than I could presumably develop parallel criticisms for work in the other disciplines as well. I would welcome comments and help from people who work in other traditions.

7. For perhaps the most useful survey of neoclassical analyses of unions see Atherton (1973: chapters 1–2).

8. For examples of the earlier literature on unions see Taft (1954) and Barbash (1967). For a crystallization of many institutionalist perspectives see Bok and Dunlop (1970). For the most formal economic analysis which incorporates institutionalist insights see Cartter (1959).

9. On the indeterminacy of the institutionalist literature see Piore (1979: editor's introduction).

10. For summaries of and references to traditional Marxian literature see Clarke and Clements (1979) and Hyman (1971; 1975).

11. I have profited enormously from Hyman's work. The major difference between his efforts and the effort represented in this essay is that I have tried to clarify the formal hypotheses of Marxian analysis at different levels of abstraction with somewhat more precision than I think he provides.

12. I work within the Marxian tradition and take its advantages over other perspectives for granted in this essay. For those who need some introduction or persuasion see Edwards *et al.* (1978) and Schwartz (1977).

13. For a little more detail on this general approach see Gordon, Edwards, and Reich (1980: chapter 1).

14. This paragraph parallels traditional Marxian discussions of abstract labor, which have always emphasized the relationship and contradictions between concrete and abstract labor. If there are any differences in my approach here, I think I emphasize the need for *continual reproduction* of the conditions necessary for abstract labor somewhat more than some traditional treatments.

15. To my knowledge this proposition about atomized labor is original. It clearly relates to others' propositions that abstract labor involves both comparability and heterogeneity of labor: I think we gain theoretical advantage by formally distinguishing between the imperative toward comparability and the imperative toward atomization because they give rise, as I argue in the following paragraphs, to partly contradictory impulses among workers. (See also Gordon, 1976.)

16. Many have focused on the possibilities for mutually beneficial and therefore harmonious bargaining between employers and employees. For Marxists the ineluctability of competition and the continuing pressure of the reserve army of labor under capitalism suggest that such cooperation, if it is ever *actually* based on mutual benefit, is likely to be short-lived.

17. This states a minimum proposition that workers will push in at least these two directions. They may, of course, be pushed in many other directions as well.

18. See Hymer (1979) for one very interesting commentary on some of these historical contradictions: his analysis is very similar to mine in many respects.

19. Trade-union structure and behavior must therefore always be modeled in analyses of the structure of *different* stages of capital accumulation. On stages of accumulation and the institutions of "labor management" and "labor market structure" see Gordon (1980).

20. By defensive I mean (somewhat more formally) those activities which people pursue to protect and advance their own interests *within* the context of and without challenging the structures which define *limits* to those activities. By offensive I mean activities which seek to transform the limits to specific activities in the pursuit of goals framing those activities. This seems to me a more useful pair of definitions than a somewhat more traditional notion that defensive actions protect against someone taking something away, while offensive activities seek to "improve" one's position. At least in the context of the capitalist/worker conflict, both sides are *always* trying to protect *and* improve their conditions. What matters is whether or not they do so through efforts to transform the structure limiting their effectiveness at pursuing those activities.

21. I develop this point further in the conclusion to this discussion of stages of accumulation. It is presented here merely for the purposes of introduction.

22. I have not provided documentation for these examples because of the space constraints on this essay. The examples are based on my informal knowledge and on other sources occasionally mentioned in the examples. I may be wrong on many of the implications

embodied in the examples. I look forward to people helping teach me more and correct my mistakes.

23. This set of comments does not imply, of course, that there will be no changes in the character of union activity from one stage of accumulation to the next. It implies, much more simply, that we cannot assume, a priori, some secular pattern of development and that each state of accumulation needs to be analyzed partly on its own terms.

24. The character of informal work groups (and other aspects of production mentioned below) are taken as exogenous factors for the purposes of this analysis, but they are obviously assumed to be at least partly endogenous to the broader process of accumulation and class struggle. For more on this argument and an application to the history of the labor process see Gordon, Edwards, and Reich (1980).

25. Although he does not base his analysis on this kind of framework, Anderson provides, for example, one study of rank-and-file participation in union activities which links their activity directly to their occupational roles and their positions within the union. See Anderson (1979).

26. There are many specific features which need to be catalogued and analyzed—variations in election procedures, grievance procedures, and so on—for which we do not yet have an adequate base of information.

27. Some specific variables could help measure this dimension: percentage of contracts rejected by the rank and file and percentage and incidence of strikes unauthorized by the leadership.

REFERENCES

Anderson, J. C. "Local Union Participation: A Re-Examination." *Industrial Relations,* winter 1979.

Ashenfelter, O., and Johnson, G. "Bargaining Theory, Trade Unions, and Strike Activity." *American Economic Review,* March 1969.

Atherton, W. N. *Theory of Union Bargaining Goals.* Princeton: Princeton University Press, 1973.

Barbash, J. *American Unions: Structure, Government, and Politics.* New York: Random House, 1967.

Bernstein, I. *The Turbulent Years.* Boston: Houghton-Mifflin, 1971.

Bok, D., and Dunlop, J. *Labor and the American Community.* New York: Simon and Schuster, 1970.

Brown, C., and Medoff, J. "Trade Unions in the Production Process." *Journal of Political Economy,* June 1978.

Cartter, A. *Theory of Wages and Employment.* Homewood, Ill.: Irwin, 1959.

Clarke, T., and Clements, L. *Trade Unions under Capitalism.* Atlantic Highlands, N.J.: Humanities Press, 1978.

Cronin, J. "Insurgencies, Strikes, and Long Cycles." In T. Hopkins and I. Wallerstein, eds., *Processes of the World-System.* Beverly Hills, Cal.: Sage Publications, 1980.

Crouch, C., and Pizzorno, A., eds. *The Analysis of Class Conflict in Western Europe.* London: Macmillan, 1978.

Edwards, R. *et al.*, eds. *The Capitalist System.* 2nd ed. Englewood Cliffs, N.J.: Prentice-Hall, 1978.

Gintis, H. "The Nature of Labor Exchange and the Theory of Capitalist Production." *Review of Radical Political Economics,* summer 1976.

Gordon, D. "Capitalist Efficiency and Socialist Efficiency." *Monthly Review,* July–August, 1976.

———. "Stages of Accumulation and Long Economic Cycles." In T. Hopkins and I. Wallerstein, eds., *Processes of the World-System.* Beverly Hills, Cal.: Sage Publications, 1980.

———, Edwards, R., and Reich, M. "The Historical Development of Labor Segmentation in the United States." In M. Reich *et al., The Segmentation of Labor in U.S. Capitalism.* New York: Cambridge University Press, 1980.

Hampton, D. R. "Factional Bargaining Patterns and Wildcat Strikes." *Human Organization,* fall 1967.

Hendricks, W. "Labor Market Structure and Union Wage Levels." *Economic Inquiry,* September 1975.

Hyman, R. *Marxism and the Sociology of Trade Unionism.* London: Pluto Press, 1971.

———. *Industrial Relations: A Marxist Introduction.* London: Macmillan, 1975.

Hymer, S. "International Politics and International Economics: A Radical Approach." In Hymer, *The Multinational Corporation: A Radical Perspective.* New York: Cambridge University Press, 1979.

Johnson, G. "The Economics of Trade Unions: A Survey of the Recent Literature." *American Economic Review,* May 1975.

Kerr, C. *et al. Industrialism and Industrial Man.* New York: McGraw-Hill, 1960.

Lerner, A. "The Economics and Politics of Consumer Sovereignty." *American Economic Review,* May 1972.

Lester, R. *As Unions Mature: An Analysis of the Evolution of American Unionism.* Princeton: Princeton University Press, 1958.

Lichtenstein. "Auto Worker Militancy and the Structure of Factory Life, 1935–1955." Unpublished paper, 1979.

Lockwood, D. *The Black-Coated Worker: A Study in Case Consciousness.* London: Allen & Unwin, 1958.

Marglin, S. "What Do Bosses Do?" *Review of Radical Political Economics,* summer 1974.

Marx, K. *The Poverty of Philosophy.* New York: International Publishers, 1963.

Peck, S. "Fifty Years after a Theory of the Labor Movement: Class Conflict in the United States." *Insurgent Sociologist,* fall 1978.

Perlman, S. *A Theory of the Labor Movement.* New York: Macmillan, 1928.

Piore, M., ed. *Unemployment and Inflation.* White Plains, N.Y.: M. E. Sharpe, 1979.

Rees, A. *The Economics of Trade Unions.* Princeton: Princeton University Press, 1962.

Ross, A. and Hartman, P. T. *Changing Patterns of Industrial Conflict.* New York: Wiley, 1960.

Sayles, L. R. *Behavior of Industrial Work Groups — Prediction and Control.* New York: McGraw-Hill, 1954.

Schwartz, J. ed. *The Subtle Anatomy of Capitalism.* Beverly Hills, Cal.: Goodyear, 1977.

Shorey, J. C., "A Quantitative Analysis of Strike Activity." *Economics,* November 1976.

Stone, K. "The Origins of Job Structures in the Steel Industry." *Review of Radical Political Economics,* summer 1974.

Strauss, G. "Factors in the Unionization of a Utilities Company." *Human Organization,* fall 1953.

Taft, P. *The Structure and Government of Labor Unions.* Cambridge, Mass.: Harvard University Press, 1954.

Thompson, E. P. *The Making of the English Working Class.* New York: Vintage Books, 1967.

Webb, S., and Webb, B. *Industrial Democracy.* London: Allen & Unwin, 1897.